Fish of Ohio

FIELD GUIDE

by **Dave Bosanko**

Adventure Publications, Inc.
Cambridge, MN

ACKNOWLEDGEMENTS

Special thanks to the U.S. Fish and Wildlife Service, and the Ohio and Minnesota Departments of Natural Resources.

Edited by Dan Johnson

Cover and book design by Jonathan Norberg

Photo/Illustration credits by artist and page number:

Cover illustrations: Walleye (main) and Bluegill (upper and back cover) by Joseph Tomelleri

Timothy Knepp/USFWS: 96, 98, 110, 112 **MyFWC.com/fishing:** 11 **Duane Raver/USFWS:** 10 (both), 11, 24, 26, 28, 30, 32, 34, 36, 42 44, 46, 50, 52, 62, 82, 92, 100, 102, 106, 130, 132, 142, 144, 148, 150 152, 154, 158, 160, 162, 168, 170, 172 **Joseph Tomelleri:** 22, 38, 40 48, 54, 56, 58, 60, 64, 66, 68, 70, 72 (both), 74 (both), 76, 78, 80, 84 86, 88, 90, 94, 96 (bottom), 102 (bottom), 104 (both), 108, 114, 116 118, 120, 122, 124, 126, 128, 134, 136, 138, 140, 146, 156, 164, 166 174, 176

10 9 8 7 6 5 4 3 2 1

Copyright 2008 by David Bosanko
Published by Adventure Publications, Inc.
820 Cleveland St. S
Cambridge, MN 55008
1-800-678-7006
www.adventurepublications.net
Printed in China
ISBN-13: 978-1-59193-079-2
ISBN-10: 1-59193-079-0

TABLE OF CONTENTS

Bowfin Family

Catfish Family

Cod Family

5

HOW TO USE THIS BOOK

Your *Fish of Ohio Field Guide* is designed to make it easy to identify more than 70 species of the most common and important fish in Ohio, and learn fascinating facts about each species' range, natural history and more.

The fish are organized by families (such as Catfish, Minnow, Perch, Pike, Salmon and Sunfish), which are listed in alphabetical order. Within these families, individual species are also arranged alphabetically, in groups where necessary. For example, members of the Sunfish family are divided into Black Bass, Crappie and True Sunfish groups. For a detailed list of fish families and individual species, turn to the Table of Contents (pg. 3); the Index (pp. 185-191) provides a handy reference guide to fish by common name (such as Lake Trout) and other common terms for the species.

Fish Identification

Determining a fish's body shape is the first step to identifying it. Each fish family usually exhibits one or sometimes two basic outlines. Catfish have long, stout bodies with flattened heads, barbels or "whiskers" around the mouth, a relatively tall but narrow dorsal fin, and an adipose fin. There are two forms of sunfish: the flat, round, plate-like outline we see in Bluegills; and the torpedo or "fusiform" shape of bass.

In this field guide you can quickly identify fish by first matching its general body shape to one of the fish family silhouettes listed in the Table of Contents (pg. 3). From there, turn to that family's section and use the illustrations and text descriptions to identify your fish. An Example

Page (pg. 22) is provided to explain how the information is presented in each two-page spread.

For some species, the illustration will be enough to identify your catch, but it is important to note that your fish may not look exactly like the picture. Fish frequently change colors. Males that are brightly colored during the spawning season may be dull silver at other times. Likewise, bass caught in muddy streams show much less pattern than those taken from clear lakes—and all fish lose some of their markings and color when they are removed from the water.

Most fish are similar in appearance to one or more other species—often, but not always, within the same family. For example, the Black Crappie is remarkably similar to its cousin the White Crappie. To accurately identify such look-alikes, check the inset illustrations and accompanying notes below the main illustration, under the "Similar Species" heading.

Throughout *Fish of Ohio*, we use basic biological and fisheries management terms that refer to physical characteristics or conditions of fish and their environment, such as "dorsal" fin or "turbid" water. For your convenience, these terms are defined in the Glossary (pg. 178), along with other handy fish-related terms and their definitions.

FISH ANATOMY

To identify fish, you will need to know a few basic terms that apply to fins and their locations.

Fins are made up of bony structures that support a membrane. There are three kinds of bony structures in fins. **Soft rays** are fixable fin supports that are sometimes branched.

Spines are stiff, often sharp supports that are not jointed. **Hard rays** are stiff, pointed, barbed structures that can be raised or lowered. Catfish are famous for their hard rays which are mistakenly called spines. Sunfish have soft rays associated with spines to form a dorsal fin.

Fins are named by their position on the fish. The **dorsal**

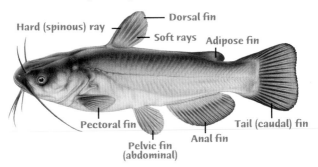

Dorsal fin
Hard (spinous) ray
Soft rays
Adipose fin
Pectoral fin
Pelvic fin (abdominal)
Anal fin
Tail (caudal) fin

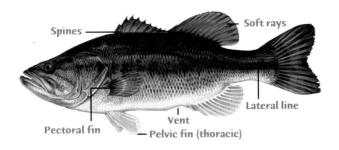

Spines
Soft rays
Pectoral fin
Vent
Pelvic fin (thoracic)
Lateral line

fin is on the top along the midline. A few fish have another fin on their back called an **adipose fin**. This is a small, fleshy protuberance located between the dorsal fin and the tail and is distinctive of trout and catfish.

On each side of the fish near the gills are the **pectoral fins**. The **anal fin** is located along the midline on the fish's bottom or ventral side. There is also a paired set of fins on the bottom of the fish called the **pelvic fins**. Pelvic fins can be in the **thoracic position** just below the pectoral fins or farther back on the stomach in the **abdominal position**. The tail is known as the **caudal fin**.

Eyes—A fish's eyes can detect color. Their eyes are rounder than those of mammals because of the refractive index of water; focus is achieved by moving the lens in and out, not distorting it as in mammals. Different species have varying levels of eyesight. Walleyes can see well in low light, while Bluegills have excellent daytime vision but see poorly at night. Catfish have bad eyes night or day.

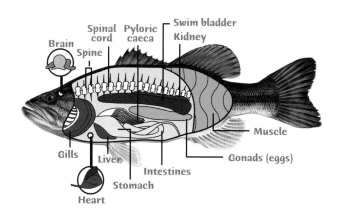

Nostrils—A pair of nostrils, or *nares*, are used to detect odors in the water. Eels and catfishes have particularly well-developed senses of smell.

Mouth—The shape of the mouth is a clue to what the fish eats. The larger the food it consumes, the larger the mouth.

Teeth—Not all fish have teeth, but those that do have mouthgear designed to help them feed. Walleyes, northern pike and muskies have sharp *canine* teeth for grabbing and holding prey. Minnows have *pharyngeal* teeth—located in the throat—for grinding. Catfish have *cardiform* teeth, which feel like a rough patch in the front of the mouth. Bass have tiny patches of *vomerine* teeth in the roof of their mouth.

Swim Bladder—Almost all fish have a swim bladder, a balloon-like organ that helps the fish regulate its buoyancy.

Lateral Line—This sensory organ helps the fish detect movement in the water (to help avoid predators or capture prey) as well as water currents and pressure changes. It consists of fluid-filled sacs with hair-like sensors, which are open to the water through a row of pores in their skin along each side—creating a visible line along the fish's side.

FISH NAMES

A Walleye is a Walleye in Ohio, where it's revered as a game fish. But in the northern parts of its range, Canadians call it a jack or jackfish. And in the eastern United States it is often called a pickerel or walleyed pike.

Because common names may vary regionally, and even change for different sizes of the same species, scientific names are used that are exactly the same around the world. Each species has only one correct scientific name that can be recognized anywhere, in any language. The Walleye is *Sander vitreus* from Cleveland to Cairo.

Scientific names are made up of Greek or Latin words that often describe the species. There are two parts to a scientific name, the generic or "genus," which is capitalized (*Sander*), and the specific name, which is not capitalized (*vitreus*). Scientific names are displayed in *italic* text.

A species' genus represents a group of closely related fish. The Walleye and the Sauger are in the same genus, so they share the generic name *Sander*. But each have different specific names, *vitreus* for Walleye, *canadense* for the Sauger.

ABOUT OHIO FISH

About 170 fish species reside in Ohio—a few more than the number found in states farther east or west. This diversity is due to the two very distinct watersheds that drain Ohio and the two major landforms that make up the state.

The southeast third of the state was not covered by ice in the last glacial period and is characterized by many small valleys with swift creeks and rivers that flow into the Ohio River. Before settlement, this area was well forested. The western part of Ohio, the glaciated part of the state, is a broad plain with prairies, rolling hills and slower, more meandering streams. This part of the state has two drainage systems. The northern part drains into Lake Erie and to the sea through the St. Lawrence River. Many of the fish in this area are species found throughout the Great

Lakes and the northern U.S. The southwestern flatlands drain into the Ohio River. The Ohio River allows fish from the southern Mississippi River drainage to reach both the southwestern prairies of Ohio and the faster streams in the unglaciated southeast.

The fish in this book represent the 30 or so species that are targeted by recreational fishermen and another 50 species that are of particular interest to those who spend time near the water, either because their status as baitfish or some unique or interesting characteristic.

FREQUENTLY ASKED QUESTIONS

What is a fish?

Fish are aquatic, cold-blooded animals with backbones, gills and fins.

Are all fish cold-blooded?

All freshwater fish are cold-blooded. Recently, it has been discovered that some members of the saltwater tuna family are warm-blooded. Whales and dolphins are also warm-blooded, but they are mammals, not fish.

Do all fish have scales?

Most fish have scales that look like the ones found on the common goldfish. A few, like gar, have scales that resemble armor plates. Some, such as catfish, have no scales at all.

How do fish breathe?

A fish takes in water through its mouth and forces it through its gills, where a system of fine membranes absorbs oxygen from the water, and releases carbon dioxide. Gills cannot pump air efficiently over these membranes, which quickly dry and stick together. Fish should never be out of the water longer than you can hold your breath.

Can fish breathe air?

Some species can; gars have a modified swim bladder that acts like a lung, allowing them to "gulp" air at the surface. Fish that can't breathe air may die when dissolved oxygen falls below critical levels, usually due to excessive rotting vegetation, and manure or chemical runoff.

How do fish swim?

Fish swim by contracting bands of muscles on alternate sides of their body, so the tail is whipped rapidly from side to side. Pectoral and pelvic fins are used for stability and steering when a fish hovers, and are sometimes used during rapid bursts of forward motion.

Do all fish look like fish?

Most do and are easily recognizable as fish. The eels and lampreys are fish, but they look like snakes. Sculpins look like little goblins with bat wings.

Where can you find fish?

Some fish species can be found in almost any body of water, but not all fish are found everywhere. Each species is adapted to exploit a particular habitat.

A species may move daily or seasonally within its home lake or stream. These movements may be horizontal, from one area to another, or vertically into deeper or shallower water.

Some are predictable seasonal migrations. In the spring, walleyes move to shallow, hard-bottom areas washed by winds or currents to spawn. Catfish frequently winter in deep holes of main rivers, and venture upstream, often into tributaries, during spring and summer.

Other movements are less predictable and are based on changing environmental conditions such as water temperature and clarity, the amount of dissolved oxygen, changes in predator or human activity, and food availability. Many fish have daily travel patterns; some predators suspend over deep water during the day, then move to structure or cover at peak feeding times.

FUN WITH FISH

There are many ways to enjoy Ohio's fish, from reading about them in this book to watching them in the wild—including donning a dive mask and jumping in; wearing polarized glasses to observe them from above the surface; or using an underwater camera to monitor fish behavior during the open-water period and through the ice.

Hands-on activities are also popular. The fishing opportunities in Ohio are incredibly numerous and diverse. From trout and salmon in the Great Lakes to sunfish off the dock—and nearly everything in between—we have it.

Proceeds from license sales, along with special taxes anglers pay on fishing supplies and motorboat fuel, fund the majority of DNR fish management efforts, including fish surveys, the development of special regulations and stocking programs. The sport also has a huge impact on Ohio's economy, supporting thousands of jobs in fishing, tourism and related industries.

CATCH-AND-RELEASE FISHING

The practices of selective harvest (keeping some fish to eat and releasing the rest) and total catch-and-release fishing allow anglers to enjoy the sport without harming the resource. Catch-and-release is especially important with certain species and sizes of fish, and in lakes or rivers where biologists are trying to improve the fishery by protecting large predators or breeding age, adult fish. The fishing regulations, DNR website and your local DNR fisheries office are excellent sources of advice on which fish to keep and which to release.

In many Ohio fisheries, trophy fish of every species are treasures too rare to be caught only once. Photographs and graphite replicas are ethical alternatives to killing a trophy fish simply for the purpose of displaying it.

Catch-and-release is only truly successful if the fish survives the experience. Following are helpful tips to help reduce the chances of post-release mortality.

- Play and land fish quickly.

- Wet your hands before touching a fish, to avoid removing its protective slime coating.

- Handle the fish gently and keep it in the water as much as possible.

- Do not hold the fish by the eyes or gills. Hold it by the lower lip or under the gill plate—and support its belly.

- If a fish is deeply hooked, cut the line so at least an inch hangs outside the mouth. This helps the hook lie flush when the fish takes in food.

- Circle hooks may help reduce the number of deeply hooked fish.

- Avoid fishing in deep water unless you plan to keep your catch.

- Don't plan to release fish that have been on a stringer or in a livewell.

FISH MEASUREMENT

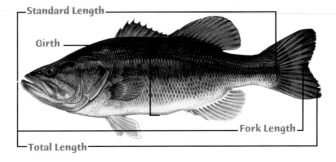

Fish are measured in three ways: standard length, fork length and total length. The first two are more accurate, because tails are often damaged or worn down. Total length is used in slot limits.

The following formulas estimate the weight of popular game fish. Lengths are in inches; weight is in pounds.

Formulas

Bass weight = (length x length x girth) / 1,200
Pike weight = (length x length x length) / 3,500
Sunfish weight = (length x length x length) / 1,200
Trout weight = (length x girth x girth) / 800
Walleye weight = (length x length x length) / 2,700

For example, let's say that you catch a 16-inch Walleye. Using the formula for Walleyes above: (16 x 16 x 16) divided by 2,700 = 1.5 pounds. Your Walleye would weigh approximately 1.5 pounds.

HELPFUL CONTACTS

Helpful fish-related contacts include:

Ohio DNR, Division of Wildlife
2045 Morse RD, Bldg. G
Columbus, OH 43229-6693
1-800-945-3543
www.dnr.state.oh.us

Fish consumption advisory
ttp://www.epa.state.oh.us/dsw/fishadvisory/

Ohio EPA, Division of Surface Water
Standards and Technical Support Section
P.O. Box 1049
Columbus, OH 43216-1049

OHIO MASTER ANGLER STATE RECORDS

Amended June, 2006. The Ohio Record fish list is maintained by the Outdoor Writers of Ohio State Record Fish Committee: http://www.outdoorwritersofohio.org

SPECIES	WEIGHT (LBS.)	WHERE CAUGHT	YEAR
Bass, Hybrid Striped	17.68	Deer Creek Lake	2001
Bass, Largemouth	13.13	Farm Pond	1976
Bass, Rock	1.97	Deer Creek near London	1932
Bass, Smallmouth	9.5	Lake Erie	1993
Bass, Spotted	5.25	Lake White	1976
Bass, Striped	37.10	West Branch Reservoir	1993
Bass, White	4	Gravel pit	1983
Bluegill	3.28	Salt Fork Reservoir	1990
Bowfin	11.69	Nettle Lake	1987
Bullhead	4.25	Farm Pond	1986
Burbot	17.33	Lake Erie	1999
Carp	50	Paint Creek	1967
Catfish, Channel	37.65	LaDue Reservoir	1992
Catfish Shovel/Flathead	76.5	Clendening Lake	1979
Crappie, Black	4.5	Private Lake	1981
Crappie, White	3.90	Private Pond	1995
Drum, Freshwater (Sheepshead)	23.5	Sandusky River	2001
Gar, Longnose	25	Ohio River	1966
Muskellunge	55.13	Piedmont Lake	1972
Muskellunge, Tiger	31.64	Turkeyfoot Lake	2006
Perch, White	1.42	Green Creek	1988
Perch, Yellow	2.75	Lake Erie	1984
Pickerel, Chain	6.25	Long Lake	1961
Pike, Northern	22.38	Lyre Lake	1988
Salmon, Chinook	29.5	Lake Erie	1989
Salmon, Coho	13.63	Huron River	1982
Salmon, Pink	3.06	Conneaut Creek	2004
Sauger	7.31	Maumee River	1981
Saugeye	14.04	Antrim Lake	2004
Sucker, Buffalo	46.01	Hoover Reservoir	1999
Sucker, (other than buffalo)	9.25	Leesville Lake	1977

SPECIES	WEIGHT (LBS.)	WHERE CAUGHT	YEAR
Sunfish, Green	.99	Farm Pond	2005
Sunfish, Hybrid	2.03	Champaign Co. Farm Pond	2003
Sunfish, Longear	.20	Big Darby Creek	2004
Sunfish, Pumpkinseed	.75	Farm pond	2001
Sunfish, Redear	3.58	Licking Co. Farm Pond	1998
Sunfish, Warmouth	1.19	LaDue Reservoir	2006
Trout, Brown	14.65	Lake Erie	1995
Trout, Lake	20.49	Lake Erie	2000
Trout, Rainbow (Steelhead)	20.97	Lake Erie	1996
Walleye	16.19	Lake Erie	1999

FISH CONSUMPTION ADVISORIES

The Ohio DNR and Department of Health have detailed information on eating fish, consumption advisories and advice on how to prepare fish to reduce risk of contaminants. Call the Department of Health, (800) 755-4769, or visit www.epa.state.oh.us/dsw/fishadvisory/.

FISH DISEASES

Fish are susceptible to parasites, infections and diseases. One of the newest threats is viral hemorrhagic septicemia (VHS). The virus, which poses no threat to humans, was found in the Great Lakes region in 2005. It caused a major die-off of perch and drum in Lake Erie in 2006, and has been linked to fish kills in lakes Huron, St. Clair and Ontario, and the St. Lawrence River. Fortunately, extensive testing of Lake Erie fish and hatchery broodstock revealed only two new cases of VHS; monitoring will likely continue for years to come. For tips on preventing the spread of VHS and invasive species visit ohioseagrant.osu.edu/research/ais/.

These pages explain how the information is presented for each fish.

SAMPLE FISH ILLUSTRATION

Description: brief summary of physical characteristics to help you identify the fish, such as coloration and markings, body shape, fin size and placement

Similar Species: lists other fish that look similar and the pages on which they can be found; also includes detailed inset drawings (below) highlighting physical traits such as markings, mouth size or shape and fin characteristics to help you distinguish this fish from similar species

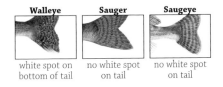

Walleye — white spot on bottom of tail

Sauger — no white spot on tail

Saugeye — no white spot on tail

SAMPLE COMPARE ILLUSTRATIONS

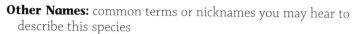
COMMON NAME
Scientific Name

Other Names: common terms or nicknames you may hear to describe this species

Habitat: environment where the fish is found (such as streams, rivers, small or large lakes, fast-flowing or still water, in or around vegetation, near shore, in clear water)

Range: geographic distribution, starting with the fish's over-all range, followed by state-specific information

Food: what the fish eats most of the time (such as crustaceans, insects, fish, plankton)

Reproduction: timing of and behavior during the spawning period (dates and water temperatures, migration information, preferred spawning habitat, type of nest if applicable, colonial or solitary nester, parental care for eggs or fry)

Average Size: average length or range of length, average weight or range of weight

Records: state—the state record for this species, location and year; North American—the North American record for this species, location and year (based on the Fresh Water Fishing Hall of Fame)

Notes: Interesting natural history information. This can be unique behaviors, remarkable features, sporting and table quality, or details on migrations, seasonal patterns or population trends.

Description: brownish-green back and sides with white belly; long, stout body; rounded tail; continuous dorsal fin; bony plates covering head; males have a large "eye" spot at the base of the tail

Similar Species: American Eel (pg. 44), Burbot (pg. 40), Sea Lamprey (pg. 58)

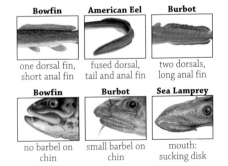

Bowfin	American Eel	Burbot
one dorsal fin, short anal fin	fused dorsal, tail and anal fin	two dorsals, long anal fin

Bowfin	Burbot	Sea Lamprey
no barbel on chin	small barbel on chin	mouth: sucking disk

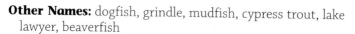

BOWFIN
Amia calva

Other Names: dogfish, grindle, mudfish, cypress trout, lake lawyer, beaverfish

Habitat: deep waters associated with vegetation in warm water lakes and rivers; feeds in shallow weed beds

Range: Mississippi River drainage east through the St. Lawrence drainage and south from Texas to Florida; in Ohio most common in the northeast bays of Lake Erie, less common in tributaries of the Ohio River

Food: fish, crayfish

Reproduction: in spring when water tops 61 degrees F, male removes vegetation to build a 2-foot nest in sand or gravel; one or more females deposits up to 5,000 eggs in nest; male tenaciously guards the nest and "ball" of young

Average Size: 12 to 24 inches, 2 to 5 pounds

Records: state—11 pounds, 11 ounces, Nettle Lake, 1987; North American—21 pounds, 8 ounces, Forest Lake, South Carolina, 1980

Notes: A voracious predator, the Bowfin prowls shallow weedbeds preying on anything that moves. Once thought detrimental to game fish populations it is now considered an asset in controlling rough fish and stunted game fish. An air breather that tolerates low oxygen levels, the Bowfin can survive buried in mud for short periods during drought conditions. Not commonly fished for or eaten in Ohio.

25

Description: black to olive-green back; sides yellowish green; belly creamy white to yellow; light bar at base of tail; barbels around mouth, dark at base; adipose fin; lacks scales; round tail

Similar Species: Brown Bullhead (pg. 28), Flathead Catfish (pg. 34), Madtom/Stonecat (pg. 38), Yellow Bullhead (pg. 30)

Black Bullhead   **Flathead Catfish**   **Black Bullhead**   **Madtom/ Stonecat**

overbite   underbite   free adipose fin   fused adipose fin

Black Bullhead   **Brown Bullhead**   **Yellow Bullhead**

olive back and sides   mottled back and sides   yellowish back and sides

BLACK BULLHEAD

Ameiurus melas

Ictaluridae

Other Names: common bullhead, horned pout

Habitat: shallow, slow-moving streams and backwaters; lakes and ponds—tolerates extremely turbid (cloudy) conditions

Range: southern Canada through the Great Lakes and the Mississippi River watershed into Mexico and the Southwest; western Pennsylvania

Food: a scavenging opportunist; feeds mostly on animal material (dead or alive) but will eat plant matter

Reproduction: spawns from late April to early June; builds nest in shallow water with a muddy bottom; both sexes guard nest, eggs and young to 1 inch in size

Average Size: 8 to 10 inches, 4 ounces to 1 pound

Records: state (unspecific bullhead)—4 pounds, 4 ounces, private pond, 1986; North American—8 pounds, 15 ounces, Sturgis Pond, Michigan, 1987

Notes: The most abundant of the three Ohio bullheads, it is the one most tolerant of silt, pollution and low oxygen levels. In Ohio the Black Bullhead has greatly increased in numbers in the past 60 years, replacing the Yellow Bullhead in many areas. Young bullheads are black, and in early summer are often seen swimming in a tight, swarming ball. Bullheads get little respect but are as tasty as, and much bigger than, most of the panfish taken home to eat.

Description: yellowish brown upper body; mottling back and sides; barbels around mouth; adipose fin; scaleless skin; rounded tail; well defined barbs on the pectoral spines

Similar Species: Black Bullhead (pg. 26), Flathead Catfish (pg. 34), Madtom/Stonecat (pg. 38), Yellow Bullhead (pg. 30)

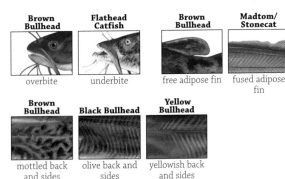

Brown Bullhead	**Flathead Catfish**	**Brown Bullhead**	**Madtom/ Stonecat**
overbite	underbite	free adipose fin	fused adipose fin

Brown Bullhead	**Black Bullhead**	**Yellow Bullhead**
mottled back and sides	olive back and sides	yellowish back and sides

BROWN BULLHEAD
Ameiurus nebulosus

Other Names: marbled or speckled bullhead, red cat

Habitat: weedy streams, lakes and sluggish streams

Range: southern Canada through the Great Lakes down the eastern states to Florida, introduced in the West; large impoundments throughout Ohio

Food: scavenging opportunist feeding mostly on insects, fish, fish eggs, snails, some plant matter

Reproduction: in early summer male builds nest in shallow water vegetation with a sand or rocky bottom; both sexes guard the eggs and young

Average Size: 8 to 10 inches, 4 ounces to 2 pounds

Records: state (unspecific bullhead)—4 pounds, 4 ounces, private pond, 1986; North American—6 pounds, 2 ounces, Pearl River, Mississippi, 1991

Notes: The Brown Bullhead is native only to the Lake Erie drainage in Ohio and, while stocked throughout the state in the early 1900s, it only became established in large impoundments. The adults are actively involved in rearing their young first by agitating the eggs then guarding the fry until they are about an inch long. Like other catfish, bull-heads are nocturnal feeders. Not highly pursued by anglers, though its reddish meat is tasty and fine table fare.

Description: olive head and back; yellowish green sides; white belly; barbels on lower jaw are pale green or white; adipose fin; scaleless skin; rounded tail

Similar Species: Black Bullhead (pg. 26), Brown Bullhead (pg. 28), Flathead Catfish (pg. 34), Madtom/Stonecat (pg. 38)

Yellow Bullhead	**Flathead Catfish**	**Yellow Bullhead**	**Madtom/ Stonecat**
overbite	underbite	free adipose fin	fused adipose fin

Yellow Bullhead	**Black Bullhead**	**Brown Bullhead**
yellowish back and sides	olive back and sides	mottled back and sides

YELLOW BULLHEAD
Ameiurus natalis

Other Names: white-whiskered bullhead, yellow cat

Habitat: warm lakes, weedy and sluggish streams

Range: southern Great Lakes through the eastern half of the U.S. to the Gulf and into Mexico, introduced in the West; throughout Ohio

Food: scavenging opportunist feeding on insects, crayfish, snails, small fish, some plant matter

Reproduction: from late spring to early summer males build nest in shallow water with some vegetation and a soft bottom; both sexes guard the eggs and young

Average Size: 8 to 10 inches, 1 to 2 pounds

Records: state (unspecific bullhead)—4 pounds, 4 ounces, private pond, 1986; North American—4 pounds, 15 ounces, Ogeechee River, Georgia, 2003

Notes: The Yellow Bullhead is not as common as the other bullheads in Ohio and the least tolerant of turbidity (cloudy water). It is more commonly found in clear streams or ponds than the other bullheads. Bullheads feed by "taste," locating food by following chemical trails through the water. This ability can be greatly diminished in polluted water, impairing the bullhead's ability to find food. The Yellow Bullhead is less likely than other bullheads to overpopulate a lake and become stunted.

31

Description: steel gray to silver on the back and sides; white belly; black spots on the sides; large fish lack spots and appear dark olive or slate gray; forked tail; adipose fin; long barbels around mouth

Similar Species: Bullheads (pp. 26-31), Flathead Catfish (pg. 34), White Catfish (pg. 36)

Channel Catfish	**Bullheads**	**Flathead Catfish**	**White Catfish**
deeply forked tail	tail rounded or slightly notched	square tail	forked tail, pointed lobes

Channel Catfish	**White Catfish**
24 to 30 rays in anal fin	22 to 24 rays in anal fin

CHANNEL CATFISH

Ictalurus punctatus

Ictaluridae

Other Names: spotted, speckled or silver catfish

Habitat: prefers clean, fast-moving streams with deep pools; stocked in many lakes; can tolerate turbid (cloudy) backwaters

Range: southern Canada through the Midwest to the Gulf of Mexico into Mexico and Florida; widely introduced across the U.S.; common throughout Ohio

Food: insects, crustaceans, fish, some plant debris

Reproduction: in early summer male builds nest in dark sheltered area such as undercut bank or log; female deposits gelatinous eggs; male guards the eggs and young until the nest is deserted

Average Size: 12 to 20 inches, 3 to 4 pounds

Records: state—37 pounds, 10 ounces, LaDue Reservoir, 1992; North American—58 pounds, Santee Cooper Reservoir, South Carolina, 1964

Notes: A highly respected sportfish in Ohio, the Channel Catfish can put up a strong fight and is fine table fare. Commonly stocked in both public and private lakes. Like other catfish, channels are nocturnal and are most successfully fished for at night. Channel Catfish were the first widely farmed fish in the U.S. and are now common in grocery stores and restaurants throughout the country.

Description: color variable, usually mottled yellow or brown; belly cream to yellow; adipose fin; chin barbels; lacks scales; tail squared; head broad and flattened; pronounced underbite

Similar Species: Bullheads (pp. 26-31), Channel Catfish (pg. 32), White Catfish (pg. 36)

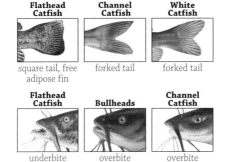

Flathead Catfish	Channel Catfish	White Catfish
square tail, free adipose fin	forked tail	forked tail

Flathead Catfish	Bullheads	Channel Catfish
underbite	overbite	overbite

FLATHEAD CATFISH

Ictaluridae

Pylodictis olivaris

Other Names: shovelnose, shovelhead; yellow, mud, pied or Mississippi cat

Habitat: deep pools of large rivers and impoundments

Range: the Mississippi River watershed and into Mexico, large rivers in the southwest; in Ohio, the Ohio River and larger tributaries, large impoundments, rarely Lake Erie

Food: fish, crayfish

Reproduction: spawns when water is 72 to 80 degrees F; male builds and defends nest in hollow log, undercut bank or other sheltered area (high preferences for cavities), large females may lay up to 30,000 eggs

Average Size: 20 to 30 inches, 10 to 20 pounds

Records: state—76 pounds, 8 ounces, Clendening Lake, 1979; North American—123 pounds, Elk City Reservoir, Kansas, 1998

Notes: A large, solitary predator that feeds aggressively on live fish, often at night. Frequently found near logjams or in deep pools. Flatheads have been introduced into a few lakes in an attempt to control stunted panfish populations. A strong, tenacious fighter with firm, white flesh.

Description: bluish-silver body and off-white belly; older
fish dark blue with some mottling; forked tail with pointed
lobes; lacks scales; adipose fin; white chin barbels

Similar Species: Bullheads (pp. 26-31), Channel Catfish (pg.
32), Flathead Catfish (pg. 34)

White Catfish	Channel Catfish	Flathead Catfish
moderately forked tail, rounded lobes	deeply forked tail, pointed lobes	square tail

White Catfish	Channel Catfish
22 to 24 rays in anal fin	24 to 30 rays in anal fin

WHITE CATFISH

Ameiurus catus

Other Names: whitey, silver or weed catfish

Habitat: freshwater to slightly brackish water coastal streams and lakes

Range: Maine south to Florida and west to Texas, introduced in some western states; introduced into lakes, ponds and streams throughout Ohio including Lake Erie

Food: insects, crayfish, small fish, and plant debris

Reproduction: male builds nest in sheltered area with a sand or gravel bottom when water temperatures reach the high 60s F; both sexes guard nest and eggs until fry disperse

Average Size: 10 to 18 inches, 1 to 2 pounds

Records: state—none; North American—22 pounds, William Land Park Lake, California, 1994

Notes: During the 1930s and '40s White Catfish were stocked in Lake Erie and fee-fishing ponds across Ohio without becoming established. More recent stockings and escapes have been more successful and White Catfish are now scattered throughout the state. They seem to be intermediate between Channel Catfish and bullheads in habits. White Catfish frequent the edge of reed beds and are often caught when still fishing the bottom near deep water. Not thought of as great sportfish, but they do have firm flesh and fine flavor.

STONECAT

TADPOLE MADTOM

Description: Tadpole Madtom—dark olive to brown; dark line on side; large, fleshy head; Stonecat—similar but lacks dark stripe, and has protruding upper jaw; both species have adipose fin continuous with tail

Similar Species: Bullheads (pp. 26-31), Catfish (pp. 32-37)

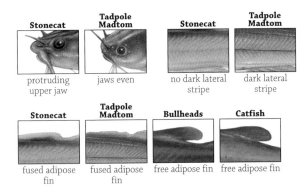

Stonecat	Tadpole Madtom	Stonecat	Tadpole Madtom
protruding upper jaw	jaws even	no dark lateral stripe	dark lateral stripe

Stonecat	Tadpole Madtom	Bullheads	Catfish
fused adipose fin	fused adipose fin	free adipose fin	free adipose fin

STONECAT *Noturus flavus*
TADPOLE MADTOM *Noturus gyrinus*

Other Name: willow cat

Habitat: weedy water near shore in medium to large lakes, under rocks in stream riffles

Range: Eastern U.S.; both widespread in Ohio

Food: small invertebrates, algae and other plant matter

Reproduction: spawning in late spring; female lays eggs under objects such as roots, rocks, logs or in abandoned crayfish burrows; nest guarded by one parent

Average Size: Tadpole Madtom—3 to 4 inches; Stonecat—4 to 6 inches

Records: none

Notes: Small, secretive fish most active at night. Both species have poison glands under the skin at the base of the dorsal and pectoral fins. Though not lethal, the poison produces a painful burning sensation, reputed to bring even the hardiest anglers to their knees. Stonecats, and to a lesser extent madtoms, are a common baitfish in some areas. Reportedly, damaging the "slime" coating (by rolling them in sand) to make handling easier will reduce their effectiveness as bait.

Description: mottled brown with creamy chin and belly; eel-like body; small barbel at each nostril opening; longer barbel on chin; long dorsal fin similar in shape and just above anal fin

Similar Species: American Eel (pg. 44), Bowfin (pg. 24), Sea Lamprey (pg. 58)

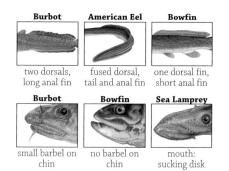

Burbot	**American Eel**	**Bowfin**
two dorsals, long anal fin	fused dorsal, tail and anal fin	one dorsal fin, short anal fin

Burbot	**Bowfin**	**Sea Lamprey**
small barbel on chin	no barbel on chin	mouth: sucking disk

BURBOT
Lota lota

Other Names: lawyer, eelpout, ling, cusk

Habitat: deep, cold, clear, rock-bottomed lakes and streams

Range: northern North America into Siberia and across northern Europe; Lake Erie in Ohio

Food: primarily small fish, but renowned for attempting to eat almost anything including fish eggs, clams and crayfish

Reproduction: pairs to large groups spawn together in mid- to late winter under the ice over a sand or gravel bottom in less than 15 feet of water; after spawning, thrashing adults scatter fertilized eggs; no nest is built and there is no parental care

Average Size: 20 inches, 2 to 8 pounds

Records: state—17 pounds, 5 ounces, Lake Erie, 1999; North American—22 pounds, 8 ounces, Little Athapapuskow Lake, Manitoba, 1994

Notes: Burbots are coldwater fish, seldom found in fisheries where the water temperature routinely exceeds 69 degrees F. It is popular with ice fishermen in some western states and Scandinavia but not highly regarded in Ohio, despite its firm, white, good-tasting flesh.

Description: gray back with purple or bronze reflections; silver sides; white underbelly; humped back; dorsal fin extends from hump to near tail; lateral line runs from head through tail

Similar Species: White Bass (pg. 168)

Freshwater Drum	**White Bass**	**Freshwater Drum**	**White Bass**
triangular tail	forked tail	down-turned mouth	upturned mouth

FRESHWATER DRUM

Aplodinotus grunniens

Other Names: sheepshead, croaker, thunderpumper, grinder, bubbler (commercially marketed as white perch)

Habitat: slow-to moderate-current areas of rivers and streams; shallow lakes with soft bottoms; prefers turbid (cloudy) water

Range: Canada south through Midwest into eastern Mexico to Guatemala; widespread in Ohio

Food: small fish, insects, crayfish, clams

Reproduction: in May and June after water temperatures reach about 66 degrees F, schools of drum lay eggs near the surface in open water over sand or gravel; no parental care of fry

Average Size: 10 to 14 inches, 2 to 5 pounds

Records: state—23 pounds, 8 ounces, Sandusky River, 2001, 1994; North American—54 pounds, 8 ounces, Nickajack Lake, Tennessee, 1972

Notes: The only freshwater member of a large family of marine fish. Named for a grunting noise that is made by males, primarily to attract females. This noise is occasionally made when a drum is removed from the water and handled. The sound is produced by specialized muscles, rubbed along the swim bladder. The skull contains two enlarged L-shaped earstones called otoliths, once prized for jewelry by Native Americans. The flesh is flaky white and tasty but easily dries out when cooked due to the low oil content.

43

Description: dark brown on top with yellow sides and white belly; long, snake-like body with large mouth, pectoral fins and gill slits; a continuous dorsal, tail and anal fin

Similar Species: Bowfin (pg. 24), Burbot (pg. 40), Sea Lamprey (pg. 58)

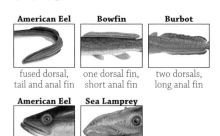

American Eel	Bowfin	Burbot
fused dorsal, tail and anal fin	one dorsal fin, short anal fin	two dorsals, long anal fin

American Eel	Sea Lamprey
mouth: jaws	mouth: sucking disk

AMERICAN EEL

Anguilla rostrata

Other Names: common, Boston, Atlantic or freshwater eel

Habitat: soft bottoms of medium to large streams, brackish tidewater areas

Range: Atlantic Ocean, eastern and central North America and eastern Central America; once common throughout Ohio, now rare

Food: insects, crayfish, small fish

Reproduction: a "catadromous" species spending most of its life in freshwater, returning to the Sargasso Sea in the North Atlantic Ocean to spawn; females lay up to 20 million eggs; adults die after spawning

Average Size: 24 to 36 inches, 1 to 3 pounds

Records: state—none; North American—8 pounds, 8 ounces, Cliff Pond, Massachusetts, 1992

Notes: Leaf-shaped larval eels drift with ocean currents for about a year. When they reach river mouths of North and Central America they morph into small eels (elvers). Males remain in the estuaries; females migrate upstream. At maturity (up to 20 years of age) adults return to the Sargasso Sea. Before the opening of the Welland Canal and being stocked by the Ohio Fish Commission in the 1880s, eels were rare in Ohio but soon became very common. They are no longer stocked and are once again rare in Ohio.

Description: olive to brown with dark spots along sides; long, cylindrical profile; single dorsal fin located just above the anal fin; body encased in hard, plate-like scales; snout twice as long as head; needlesharp teeth on both jaws

Similar Species: Shortnose, Spotted Gar, both rare in state

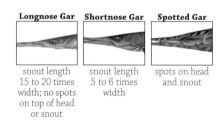

Longnose Gar	Shortnose Gar	Spotted Gar
snout length 15 to 20 times width; no spots on top of head or snout	snout length 5 to 6 times width	spots on head and snout

LONGNOSE GAR

Lepisosteus osseus

Other Names: garfish

Habitat: quiet water of larger rivers and lakes

Range: central U.S. throughout the Mississippi drainage south into Mexico, a few rivers in the Northeast in the Great Lakes drainage; in Ohio, larger streams of the Ohio River drainage, Lake Erie and associated streams

Food: minnows and other small fish

Reproduction: large, green eggs are laid in weedy shallows when water temperatures reach the high 60s F; using a small disk on the snout, newly hatched gar attach to something solid until their digestive tracts develop enough to begin feeding

Average Size: 1 to 3 feet, 2 to 5 pounds

Records: state—25 pounds, Ohio River, 1966; North American—50 pounds, 5 ounces, Trinity River, Texas, 1954

Notes: Gars belong to a prehistoric family of fish that can breathe air with the aid of a modified swim bladder. This makes them well suited to survive in our increasingly polluted, slow-moving rivers and lakes. Gars are a valuable asset in controlling growing populations of rough fish in these waters. The Longnose Gar is the only gar that is commonly found in Ohio. The Spotted and Shortnose Gar had restricted ranges and are now endangered, if present at all. The huge Alligator Gar was occasionally caught in the lower Ohio River through the early 1900s.

Description: dark gray body with black or brown blotches; divided dorsal fin with green border; black spot at base of front dorsal fin; pelvic fin fused to form sucker-like disk; large head with rapidly tapering body

Similar Species: Mottled Sculpin (pg. 118)

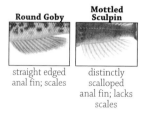

Round Goby	Mottled Sculpin
straight edged anal fin; scales	distinctly scalloped anal fin; lacks scales

ROUND GOBY

Neogobius melanostomus

Other Names: ship or tank goby

Habitat: bottom dweller of rocky or weedy shorelines in large, clear lakes; favors deep water during winter

Range: native to the Black and Caspian seas; in Ohio, Lake Erie

Food: mollusks, crustaceans, fish eggs, small fish

Reproduction: long spawning season from late spring through early summer; males spread a sticky substance on the undersides of logs or rocks, on which the females attach eggs; several females may use the same nest; males guard the nests and may die after spawning season

Average Size: 4 to 5 inches

Records: none

Notes: Gobies are an invasive species that were transported from Eurasia in ballast water of ocean going ships. A secretive fish that hides under rocks or buries itself in sand. A voracious feeder and prolific breeder, gobies are spreading rapidly in the Great Lakes, threatening native species. The only plus to this species is that an adult can consume 30 to 50 zebra mussels in a day.

Description: blue to blue-green metallic back; silver sides with faint dark stripes; white belly; purple spot just behind the gill directly above the pectoral fin; large mouth with protruding lower jaw; sharply pointed scales (scutes) along the ventral midline

Similar Species: Gizzard Shad (pg. 54), Skipjack Herring (pg. 52)

Alewife

lower jaw
protrudes
beyond snout

Gizzard Shad

snout
protrudes over
mouth

Alewife

purple spot
behind upper
edge of gill

Skipjack Herring

no spot behind
upper edge
of gill

ALEWIFE

Alosa pseudoharengus

Other Names: ellwife, sawbelly, golden shad, big-eyed herring, river herring

Habitat: open water of the Great Lakes and a few inland lakes; coastal waters and streams

Range: Atlantic Ocean from Labrador to the Carolinas, St. Lawrence River drainage and Great Lakes; Lake Erie in Ohio

Food: zooplankton, filamentous algae

Reproduction: in the Great Lakes, spawning takes place in open water of bays and protected shorelines during early summer; coastal alewives make spring runs up rivers when the water warms to 50 degrees F to spawn over sandy bottoms in protected bays

Average Size: landlocked—4 to 8 inches; marine—12 to 15 inches, 1 pound

Records: none

Notes: Alewives were first seen in Lake Ontario in the 1870s and first recorded in Lake Erie in September 1931. With the Sea Lamprey introduction and the decline of Lake Trout the Alewife population exploded. With the controlling of Sea Lampreys, introduction of salmon and recovering Lake Trout populations, the Alewife has now become the base for the Great Lakes sportfishery. Alewives are not well suited to warm, freshwater impoundments and occasionally have late summer die-offs, then wash up on the shore to the disgust of beach goers.

Description: deep, laterally compressed silver body with a blue-green back that ends abruptly, not shading into sides; no dark spots on the shoulder; saw-tooth edge of sharply pointed scales along belly (scutes)

Similar Species: Alewife (pg. 50), Gizzard Shad (pg. 54)

Skipjack Herring	**Alewife**	**Skipjack Herring**	**Gizzard Shad**
blue-green back ends abruptly at silver sides	gray-green back shades to silver	no long thread on last ray of dorsal fin	long thread on last dorsal ray

Skipjack Herring	**Alewife**	**Gizzard Shad**
no spot behind upper edge of gill	single dark spot behind upper edge of gill	spot behind upper edge of gill

SKIPJACK HERRING

Alosa chrysochloris

Other Names: river herring, skipper

Habitat: the clearer water in large rivers, often at the mouth of tributary streams and below dams

Range: Gulf Coast waters from Texas to Florida, the Mississippi River and its large tributaries and impoundments; in Ohio, the Ohio and Scioto rivers

Food: small fish, insects

Reproduction: little is known about spawning, but seems to spawn in early spring as individuals or in small schools in clear water near the mouth of tributary streams

Average Size: 12 to 16 inches, 1 to 2 pounds

Records: state—none; North American—3 pounds, 12 ounces, Watts Bar Lake, Tennessee, 1982

Notes: The Skipjack Herring is a very fast fish that often leaps out of the water as it chases prey. It got its name for its spectacular skips across the water. Skipjacks are fish of big rivers, not often entering smaller tributaries. They feed at the surface and prefer the clear, less turbid (cloudy) parts of the river. Skipjacks readily take flies and small lures, and on light tackle are one of Ohio's most sporting fish.

Description: deep laterally compressed body; silvery blue back with white sides and belly; younger fish have a dark spot on shoulder behind gill; small mouth; last rays of dorsal fin form a long thread

Similar Species: Alewife (pg. 50), Skipjack Herring (pg. 52)

Gizzard Shad

snout protrudes over mouth

Alewife

lower jaw protrudes beyond snout

Gizzard Shad

last ray of dorsal fin extending into long thread

Alewife

last ray of dorsal fin doesn't extend into long thread

Gizzard Shad

spot behind upper edge of gill

Skipjack Herring

no spot behind upper edge of gill

GIZZARD SHAD

Dorosoma cepedianum

Other Names: hickory, mud or jack shad

Habitat: large rivers, reservoirs, lakes, swamps and temporarily flooded pools; brackish and saline waters in coastal areas

Range: St. Lawrence and Great Lakes, Mississippi, Atlantic and Gulf Slope drainages from Quebec to Mexico, south to central Florida; common throughout Ohio

Food: herbivorous filter feeder

Reproduction: spawning takes place in tributary streams and along lakeshores in early summer; schooling adults release eggs in open water without regard to individual mates

Average Size: 6 to 8 inches, 1 to 8 ounces

Records: state—none; North American—4 pounds, 12 ounces, Lake Oahe, South Dakota, 2006

Notes: The Gizzard Shad is a widespread, prolific fish that is best known as forage for popular game fish. At times it can become over-abundant and experience large die-offs. The name "gizzard" refers to this shad's long, convoluted intestine that is often packed with sand. Though Gizzard Shad are a management problem at times, they form a valuable link in turning plankton into usable forage for larger game fish. Occasionally, larger Gizzard Shad are caught with hook and line, but they have little food value.

AMERICAN BROOK LAMPREY

Description: eel-like body; round, sucking-disk mouth; seven paired gill openings; dorsal fin long, extending to tail; no paired fins

Similar Species: American Eel (pg. 44), Bowfin (pg. 24), Burbot (pg. 40), Sea Lamprey (pg. 58)

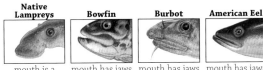

Native Lampreys	Bowfin	Burbot	American Eel
mouth is a sucking disk	mouth has jaws	mouth has jaws	mouth has jaws

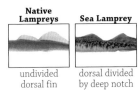

Native Lampreys	Sea Lamprey
undivided dorsal fin	dorsal divided by deep notch

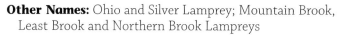

NATIVE LAMPREYS

Ichthyomyzon, Lampetra

Petromyzontidae

Other Names: Ohio and Silver Lamprey; Mountain Brook, Least Brook and Northern Brook Lampreys

Habitat: juveniles live in the quiet pools of streams and rivers; adults may move into some lakes

Range: fresh waters of eastern North America; in Ohio, the Ohio Lamprey is found in the Ohio River drainage; Silver Lamprey in the Lake Erie and Ohio River drainage; Northern and Mountain Brook Lamprey in central and east Ohio; Least Brook Lamprey in the Allegheny drainage

Food: juvenile lampreys are bottom filter feeders in streams; adults are either parasitic on fish or do not feed

Reproduction: adults build nest in the gravel of streambeds when water temperatures reach mid 50s F; die soon after spawning

Average Size: 6 to 12 inches

Records: none

Notes: Lampreys are primitive fish with skeletons made of cartilage. In Ohio there are five native lampreys. The Ohio and Silver Lamprey are parasitic in the adult form, often leaving small, round wounds on their prey. The Brook Lampreys are non-parasitic. All the native lampreys co-exist with the other Ohio fish species with little or no effect on their populations. Due to deteriorating water conditions many native lampreys are endangered or threatened throughout their range.

Description: eel-like body; round, sucking-disk mouth; seven paired gill openings; long dorsal fin extends to tail and is divided into two parts by a deep notch; no paired fins

Similar Species: American Eel (pg. 44), Bowfin (pg. 24), Burbot (pg. 40), Native Lampreys (pg. 56)

Sea Lamprey	American Eel	Bowfin	Burbot
mouth is a sucking disk	mouth has jaws	mouth has jaws	mouth has jaws

Sea Lamprey	Native Lampreys
dorsal fin divided by deep notch	undivided dorsal fin

58

SEA LAMPREY

Petromyzon marinus

Petromyzontidae

Other Names: landlocked or lake lamprey

Habitat: juveniles live in quiet pools of freshwater streams; adults are free-swimming in lakes or oceans

Range: Atlantic Ocean from Greenland to Florida, Norway to the Mediterranean; introduced into Lake Erie in Ohio

Food: juveniles are filter feeders in bottoms of freshwater streams, adults are parasitic, attaching to fish with a disk-shaped sucker mouth, then using sharp tongue to rasp through the scales and skin to feed on blood and body fluids; many "host" fish die

Reproduction: both adults build a nest in the gravel after ascending clear streams, then die shortly after spawning; young remain in the streams several years before returning to the lake or sea as adults

Average Size: 12 to 24 inches

Records: none

Notes: The Sea Lamprey is native to eastern coastal streams of North America where it coexists with native fish species with little effect on natural populations. With the completion of the Welland Canal, Sea Lampreys entered the Great Lakes with devastating results. The overfished Lake Trout and Whitefish fisheries soon collapsed. Now that Sea Lampreys are under partial control, Lake Trout have returned to at least sportfishing levels and Whitefish enough to allow moderate commercial fishing.

Description: dark gray to black back; silver-gray sides with dark blotches; low-set eyes that look down; upturned mouth; body scales tiny, none on head

Similar Species: Common Carp (pg. 62), Grass Carp (pg. 64), Silver Carp (pg. 66)

Bighead Carp

Common Carp

Grass Carp

upturned mouth
lacks barbels;
eyes low on
head

down-turned
sucker mouth
with barbels

upturned mouth
lacks barbels;
eyes in middle
of head

Bighead Carp

Silver Carp

keeled belly
from pelvic fin
to anal fin

keeled belly
from head to
anal fin

BIGHEAD CARP
Hypophthalmichthys nobilis

Other Names: river carp, lake fish, speckled amur

Habitat: large, warm rivers and connected lakes

Range: Asia, introduced in other parts of the world; in Ohio, the Ohio River and larger tributaries, and lakes in the Ohio River floodplain

Food: aquatic vegetation and floating plankton, mostly algae

Reproduction: spawns from late spring to early summer in warm, flowing water

Average Size: 24 to 36 inches, 5 to 50 pounds

Records: state—none; North American—90 pounds, Kirby Lake, Texas, 2000

Notes: Bighead Carp are the fourth most important aquaculture fish in the world. They were introduced to the U.S. to control algae in southern aquaculture ponds and are now commonly farmed as a dual crop with catfish. They escaped to the Mississippi River and are now well established in the Ohio River and the predominant fish in some areas. The Silver Carp, and to a lesser degree the Bighead Carp, make high leaps from the water when frightened by boats. As filter feeders Bighead Carp are targets for bow fishermen but not anglers. They have a pleasant, mild flavor but are bony and are not highly regarded table fare in this country.

Description: brassy yellow to golden brown or dark olive back and sides; white to yellow belly; two pairs of barbels near round, extendable mouth; red tinged tail and anal fin; each scale has a dark spot at base and dark margin

Similar Species: Bighead Carp (pg. 60)

Common Carp	**Bighead Carp**	**Common Carp**	**Bighead Carp**
down-turned mouth with barbels; eyes high on head	upturned mouth lacks barbels; eyes low on head	large body scales	body scales tiny

COMMON CARP

Cyprinus carpio

Other Names: German, European, mirror or leather carp, buglemouth

Habitat: warm, shallow, quiet, weedy waters of streams and lakes

Range: native to Asia, introduced worldwide; common throughout Ohio

Food: opportunistic feeder, prefers insect larvae, crustaceans and mollusks, but at times eats algae and some higher plants

Reproduction: spawns from late spring to early summer in very shallow water at stream and lake edges; very obvious when spawning with a great deal of splashing

Average Size: 16 to 18 inches, 5 to 20 pounds

Records: state—50 pounds, Paint Creek, 1967; North American—57 pounds, 13 ounces, Tidal Basin, Washington D.C., 1983

Notes: One of the world's most important freshwater species, the fast-growing carp provides sport and food for millions of people throughout its range. This Asian minnow was introduced into Europe in the twelfth century but didn't make it to North America until the 1800s. The first fingerling carp were sent to Ohio in the fall of 1879 and by 1890 were common but not abundant in most Ohio streams. Carp are a highly prized sportfish in Europe but have not gained the same status in the U.S.

Description: olive to silver-white back and cross-hatched sides; large scales with a dark edge and black spot at base; clear to gray-brown fins; upturned mouth; no barbels

Similar Species: Bighead Carp (pg. 60), Common Carp (pg. 62), Silver Carp (pg. 66)

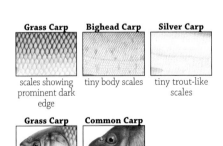

Grass Carp | **Bighead Carp** | **Silver Carp**

scales showing prominent dark edge | tiny body scales | tiny trout-like scales

Grass Carp | **Common Carp**

mouth lacks barbels | mouth has barbels

GRASS CARP

Ctenopharyngodon idella

Cyprinidae

Other Names: white amur

Habitat: lakes, ponds and backwaters of large, warm rivers

Range: Asia, introduced in other parts of the world; in Ohio, many ponds, and lakes, the Ohio River and large tributaries

Food: submerged aquatic vegetation, some floating algae

Reproduction: spawns from late spring to early summer, laying over a million eggs in warm, slowly flowing water; eggs remain suspended for several days before hatching

Average Size: 24 to 36 inches, 5 to 50 pounds

Records: state—none; North American—78 pounds, 12 ounces, Flint River, Georgia, 2003

Notes: Grass Carp were introduced into the U.S. in the 1960s for food and aquatic vegetation control. By the late '70s, escaped or captive Grass Carp could be found in 40 states. Using Grass Carp for vegetation control is still permitted and popular in many states, including Ohio, but only using non-breeding (triploid) fish. Grass Carp are well established in the lakes and streams of the Ohio River basin. They are more often hooked than the other Asian carp but not consistently enough to be of interest to anglers.

Description: dark green back; silver sides with a cross-hatched pattern; upturned mouth; eyes far forward and low on head; tiny trout-like scales; no head scales

Similar Species: Bighead Carp (pg. 60), Common Carp (pg. 62), Grass Carp (pg. 64)

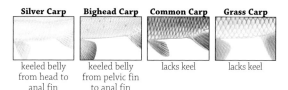

Silver Carp	Bighead Carp	Common Carp	Grass Carp
keeled belly from head to anal fin	keeled belly from pelvic fin to anal fin	lacks keel	lacks keel

SILVER CARP

Hypophthalmichthys molitrix

Other Names: shiner carp

Habitat: quiet waters of large, warm rivers and connected lakes and ponds

Range: Asia, introduced in other parts of the world; in Ohio the Ohio River, large tributaries and lakes in the Ohio River floodplain

Food: aquatic vegetation, some floating algae

Reproduction: spawns from late spring to early summer in off-current and backwaters of large to midsized streams

Average Size: 24 to 36 inches, 5 to 50 pounds

Records: none

Notes: Silver Carp were introduced to Arkansas in the early 1970s to control algae in aquaculture ponds and sewage lagoons, then escaped to the Mississippi River. Breeding populations are well established in the Ohio River and adjoining lakes. Combined with Bighead Carp they are the predominant fish in some areas and together are having a devastating effect on river ecology. The Silver Carp, and to a lesser degree the Bighead Carp, make high leaps from the water when frightened by boats. As algae feeders they are targets for bow fishermen but not anglers. They have limited food value in this country.

Description: dark olive back; silver-gray sides that reflect purple; large mouth; dark spot at base of dorsal fin; small barbel that fits in a grove between the back of the upper jaw and snout (very evident when the mouth is opened)

Similar Species: Fallfish, Fathead Minnow (pg. 72)

Creek Chub	**Fallfish**	**Creek Chub**	**Fallfish**
dark spot at front of dorsal	no dark spot at base of dorsal	rounded tail	tail sharply pointed

Creek Chub	**Fathead Minnow**
mouth extends to eye	mouth does not extend to eye

CREEK CHUB
Semotilus atromaculatus

Other Names: common, brook, silver, mud or blackspot chub, horned or northern horned dace

Habitat: primarily found in quiet pools in clear streams and rivers, occasionally in lakes

Range: Montana south through the Gulf States; common throughout Ohio

Food: small aquatic invertebrates, and crustaceans

Reproduction: in late spring male excavates a 1- to 3-foot long, teardrop shaped pit at the head of stream riffles; using its mouth or rolling stones with its head, male fills pit to 6 to 8 inches high; females lay eggs on the mound, which are then covered and defended by male; several other species spawn on the mounds, occasionally resulting in hybridization

Average Size: 4 to 10 inches, up to 8 ounces

Records: none

Notes: The Creek Chub is one of the most common stream fishes in eastern North America. They take bait readily and are often fished for by kids spending a day on the creek. When water levels are low in late summer, the chub spawning mounds can be plentiful and quite evident, leaving many passersby to speculate on their origin. Chubs are a highly prized bait minnow, and local populations can be easily depleted by overharvesting.

Description: dark green, blotchy back; sides with two broad lateral bands on tan background; creamy red between stripes; yellow belly; in breeding males belly turns bright red; in females, belly turns yellow-orange but never red, scales very small

Similar Species: Northern Redbelly Dace—rare in Ohio

Southern Redbelly Dace	**Northern Redbelly Dace**
curved mouth, upper jaw slightly ahead of the lower	curved mouth, lower jaw slightly ahead of the upper

SOUTHERN REDBELLY DACE

Cyprinidae

Phoxinus erythrogaster

Other Names: redbelly or yellow-belly dace, leatherback

Habitat: small, clear streams with wooded and undercut banks

Range: north-central U.S. with outlying populations in the Ozark Mountains; southeastern two-thirds of Ohio

Food: bottom feeders on algae and broken vegetation particles

Reproduction: in early summer a single female attended by two males or mixed schools spawns near the bottom among pebbles in slow-moving pools; eggs hatch in 8 to 10 days without parental care

Average Size: 2 to 3 inches

Records: none

Notes: A small group of minnows in Ohio are referred to as daces. These small fish are primarily stream dwellers. The brightly colored Southern Redbelly Dace is one of Ohio's most beautiful fish and well suited to be an aquarium fish. If the light is controlled they will maintain their breeding colors for several months. Dace congregate in tightly packed schools when water levels are low, making them very susceptible to predators and overharvesting for bait.

NON-SPAWNING ADULT

SPAWNING MALE

Description: olive to slate-gray back; dull golden yellow sides; dark side stripe narrows toward tail then widens to dark spot; rounded snout and fins; no scales on head; dark blotch on front of dorsal fin

Similar Species: Creek Chub (pg. 68)

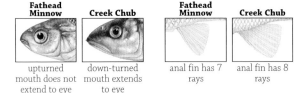

Fathead Minnow	Creek Chub	Fathead Minnow	Creek Chub
upturned mouth does not extend to eye	down-turned mouth extends to eye	anal fin has 7 rays	anal fin has 8 rays

FATHEAD MINNOW

Pemephales promelas

Other Names: fathead, blackhead minnow; tuffy

Habitat: shallow pools of midsize to small streams, shallow, weedy lakes and ponds

Range: east of the Rocky Mountains in the U.S. and Canada; common in all Ohio watersheds

Food: primarily plant matter, some insects and copepods

Reproduction: male prepares nest beneath rocks and sticks; female enters and turns upside down to lay adhesive eggs on overhang; male fans the eggs and massages them with a special mucus-like pad on its back

Average Size: 3 to 4 inches

Records: none

Notes: There are more than 40 species of minnows found in Ohio, over 200 known from North America and 1,500 in the world. The carps and goldfish are minnows that were introduced from Asia. Native minnows are small fish ranging from a few inches to a foot long. The Fathead Minnow is one of Ohio's most numerous and widespread fish. It and the Bluntnose Minnow are the common bait minnows and are certainly two of the most economically important fish in the U.S.

COMMON SHINER

GOLDEN SHINER

Description: silver body with dark green back, often with light body stripe; breeding males have bluish heads and rosy pink body and fins

Similar Species: Creek Chub (pg. 68), Golden Shiner

Common Shiner	**Creek Chub**	**Common Shiner**	**Golden Shiner**
mouth barely extends to eye, which is large in relation to head	mouth extends almost to middle of eye, which is small in relation to head	8 to 10 rays on anal fin (usually 9)	11 to 15 rays on anal fin

COMMON SHINER

Luxilus cornutus

Cyprinidae

Other Names: eastern, creek or redfin shiner

Habitat: lakes, rivers and streams; most common in pools of cool, clear streams

Range: Midwest through eastern U.S. and Canada; common in all Ohio watersheds

Food: small aquatic insects, zooplankton, algae

Reproduction: male prepares nest of small stones at the head of stream riffles, (sometimes using the nest of Creek or Hornyhead Chubs); male courts females with great flourish, then guards the nest, sometimes in conjunction with Hornyhead Chub

Average Size: 4 to 12 inches

Records: none

Notes: There are almost twenty Ohio minnows called shiners and most are in the genus *Notropis*. Not all shiners are as flashy as the name indicates; some have a dull coloration and show almost no silver on the sides. The Common Shiner is a large, showy fish that has now replaced the Golden Shiner as the common bait shiner though it seems somewhat less hardy on the line. Large Common Shiners can be caught with dry flies and can be very sporting on light tackle but are not meaty enough to put on the table.

Description: dark green to dark blue back and upper sides; bright silver or golden sides; large yellow-tinged eye; large scales; thin body flattened from side to side with a sharp scale ridge (keel) from throat to pelvic fin

Similar Species: Gizzard Shad (pg. 54), Mooneye (pg. 78), Skipjack Herring (pg. 52)

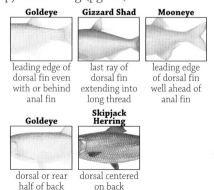

Goldeye	Gizzard Shad	Mooneye
leading edge of dorsal fin even with or behind anal fin	last ray of dorsal fin extending into long thread	leading edge of dorsal fin well ahead of anal fin

Goldeye	Skipjack Herring
dorsal or rear half of back	dorsal centered on back

GOLDEYE

Hiodon alosoides

Other Names: Winnipeg or western goldeye, toothed or yellow herring

Habitat: large lakes and quiet backwaters of large, turbid (cloudy) streams and rivers

Range: Hudson Bay drainage south through the Ohio and Mississippi drainage to Tennessee; in Ohio, the Ohio and Scioto rivers

Food: insects, small fish, crayfish, snails

Reproduction: spawning takes place in turbid pools and backwaters when water temperatures reach the mid-50s F

Average Size: 12 to 18 inches, 1 to 2 pounds

Records: state—none; North American—3 pounds, 13 ounces, Lake Oahe tailwater, South Dakota, 1987

Notes: The Goldeye's large, yellow eye is an adaptation for low-light conditions, enabling it to feed at night and navigate dark, silty waters. It feeds near the surface in quiet pools in association with Mooneyes. Harvested commercially from large Canadian lakes for 150 years, it was served on the Canadian Pacific Railway as Winnipeg Smoked Goldeye. Goldeyes readily take flies and small lures and though not often sought by anglers, are frequently caught while fishing for other species. They are still fairly common below the dams in the Ohio and Scioto rivers.

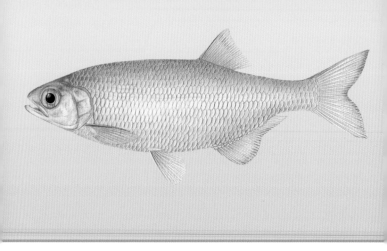

Description: olive back; silver sides; large scales on body but none on head; large white eye, over one-third width of head; thin body flattened from side to side with sharp scale-less keel between pelvic and anal fin

Similar Species: Gizzard Shad (pg. 54), Goldeye (pg. 76),

Mooneye	**Gizzard Shad**	**Goldeye**
white eye, lower jaw protrudes beyond snout	yellow eye, snout protrudes over mouth	yellowish eye, snout protrudes beyond lower jaw

MOONEYE
Hiodon tergisus

Other Names: white shad, slicker, toothed herring, river whitefish

Habitat: clear, quiet waters of large lakes and the backwaters of large streams

Range: Hudson Bay drainage east to the St. Lawrence, through the Mississippi drainage south into Arkansas and Alabama; in Ohio, Lake Erie and larger tributaries, the Ohio River and larger tributaries

Food: insects, small fish, crayfish, snails

Reproduction: adults migrate up larger tributaries to spawn in early spring when water temperatures reach mid-50s F; gelatin-coated eggs are released over gravel bars in fast current

Average Size: 12 inches, 12 ounces to 1 pound

Records: state—none; North American—1 pound, 1 ounce, Lake Poygan, Wisconsin, 2000

Notes: Mooneyes are small, beautiful, flashy fish that jump repeatedly when hooked. However, they are bony with little meat except along the back. They feed on insects near or on the surface in slack waters of large lakes and rivers. Mooneyes look like freshwater herring but are in their own family containing only two members. Once commercially harvested in some states, Mooneyes are declining over much of their range and Ohio is no exception. Though small, they are related to the Arapaima, the world's largest scaled freshwater fish.

79

Description: olive green back; tan to yellow-brown sides with faint wavy vertical bars; rounded tail; dark bar just before the tail; slightly flattened head

Similiar Species: Banded Killifish, Fathead Minnow (pg. 72)

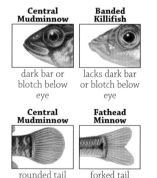

Central Mudminnow	Banded Killifish
dark bar or blotch below eye	lacks dark bar or blotch below eye

Central Mudminnow	Fathead Minnow
rounded tail	forked tail

CENTRAL MUDMINNOW

Umbra limi

Umbridae

Other Names: Mississippi or western mudminnow, dogfish, mudfish

Habitat: slow, stagnant waters of weedy streams and ponds with soft bottoms

Range: Great Lakes states through the Midwest; Lake Erie and the northeast two-thirds of Ohio

Food: insects, mollusks, larger crustaceans

Reproduction: in the early spring, adults move into flooded pools when water temperatures reach the mid-50s F; yellow-orange eggs are deposited singly on plant leaves and are left to hatch without parental care

Average Size: 2 to 4 inches

Records: none

Notes: This hardy little fish can stand very low oxygen levels and gulp air to breathe (even from air bubbles under the ice). They hide in the bottom detritus but do not bury themselves tail first in the mud as often reported. They are frequently the only fish left in ponds after winter die-offs. They are good baitfish, withstanding the bait pail and hooks well. They can be fun aquarium fish, quickly learning to eat small pieces of meat or angleworms when offered.

Description: large gray scale-less body; snout protrudes into a large paddle; shark-like forked tail; gills extend into long, pointed flaps

Similar Species: Channel Catfish (pg. 32)

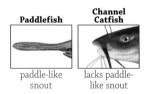

Paddlefish	**Channel Catfish**
paddle-like snout	lacks paddle-like snout

PADDLEFISH

Polyodon spathula

Other Names: spoonbill cat, duckbill

Habitat: deep pools of large rivers and their connecting lakes

Range: large rivers in the Mississippi drainage: in Ohio historically Lake Erie and Scioto River, currently the Ohio River

Food: free swimming plankton

Reproduction: spawning takes place when water levels are rising in the spring and temperatures reach the low 50s F; adults migrate up large tributaries until blocked by dams; breeding schools gather in moving water less than 10 feet deep to release eggs over large gravel bars

Average Size: 2 to 4 feet, 20 to 40 pounds

Records: state—none; North American—144 pounds, Dam No. 7, Kansas, 2004

Notes: This prehistoric fish is very shark-like in anatomy, with its only close relative found in the Yangtze River of China. Paddlefish have a large mouth but no teeth and feed entirely on plankton. The function of the paddle is not well understood but it is not used to dig in the mud. Scientists believe that sensors in the paddle detect electrical currents created by clouds of plankton. The construction of locks and dams has greatly reduced the Paddlefish population in most of the state. There is a small population of Paddlefish in the Ohio River and a stocking program is underway.

Description: tan to olive back and upper sides with dark blotches and speckling; sides tan to golden with X, Y and W patterns; breeding males dark with black bars

Similar Species: Trout-perch (pg. 176)

Johnny Darter	Trout-perch
lacks adipose fin	adipose fin

Percidae

JOHNNY DARTER

Etheostoma nigrum

Other Names: red-sided, yellowbelly or weed darter

Habitat: lakes that have some vegetation or algae mat; clear, slow-flowing streams

Range: Rocky Mountains east across Canada and the U.S. through the Great Lakes region; widespread in Ohio

Food: small aquatic invertebrates

Reproduction: in May and June, males migrate to shorelines to establish breeding areas; females move from territory to territory, spawning with several males; each sequence produces 7 to 10 eggs that attach to the bottom

Average Size: 2 to 4 inches

Records: no record

Notes: Relatives of Yellow Perch and Walleyes, darters are primarily stream fish adapted to living among the rocks in fast current. A small swim bladder allows darters to sink rapidly to the bottom after a "dart," thus avoiding being swept away by the current. Darters are hard to see when they move but are easy to spot when perched on their pectoral fins. Johnny Darters prefer weedy lake shorelines but can be found in a large range of habitats.

Description: slender body; gray to dark silver or yellowish brown with dark blotches on sides; black spots on spiny dorsal fin; may exhibit some white on lower margin of tail, but lacks prominent white tail spot found on Walleye

Similar Species: Saugeye (pg. 88), Walleye (pg. 90)

Sauger	Saugeye	Walleye
spiny dorsal fin is spotted, lacks dark blotch on rear base	spiny dorsal fin with distinct spots, dark spot on rear base	spiny dorsal lacks indistinct streaks or blotches, spot on rear base
Sauger	**Saugeye**	**Walleye**
no white spot on tail	rounded tail, no white spot on bottom of tail	white spot on bottom of tail

SAUGER

Sander canadensis

Other Names: sand, spotfin or river pike, jackfish, jack salmon

Habitat: large lakes and rivers

Range: large lakes in southern Canada, northern U.S. and the larger reaches of the Mississippi, Missouri, Ohio and Tennessee river drainages; in Ohio, the Ohio River, Lake Erie and its tributaries

Food: small fish, aquatic insects, crayfish

Reproduction: spawns in April and May as water approaches 50 F; adults move into the shallow waters of tributaries and headwaters to randomly deposit eggs over gravel beds

Average Size: 10 to 12 inches, 8 ounces to 2 pounds

Records: state—7 pounds, 5 ounces, Maumee River, 1981; North American—8 pounds, 12 ounces, Lake Sakakawea, North Dakota, 1971

Notes: Though the Sauger is the Walleye's smaller cousin it is a big-water fish residing primarily in large lakes and rivers. It is slow growing, often reaching only two pounds in 20 years. It is an important sportfish summer and winter in Lake Erie though populations in the Ohio River have been greatly reduced in recent years. The Sauger is an aggressive daytime feeder compared to Walleye. Its fine-flavored flesh is top table fare.

Description: slender body; gray to dark silver or yellowish brown with dark blotches on sides; two dorsal fins, front spiny, rear with soft rays; black spots on spiny dorsal fin; lacks prominent white tail spot found on Walleye

Similar Species: Sauger (pg. 86), Walleye (pg. 90)

Saugeye	**Sauger**	**Walleye**
spiny dorsal fin with distinct streaks; dark spot on rear base	spiny dorsal fin is spotted, lacks dark blotch on rear base	spiny dorsal fin lacks spots, has large dark blotch on rear base

Saugeye	**Walleye**
no white spot on bottom of tail	white spot on bottom of tail

SAUGEYE

Sander vitreus x Sander canadensis

Other Names: saugie, rivereye

Habitat: stocked in lakes, reservoirs and streams; may become established below dams

Range: hatchery produced fish stocked in Midwest and West; in Ohio, commonly stocked in lakes and rivers

Food: mainly small fish, but also eats insects, crayfish

Reproduction: spawning behavior similar to Walleye and Sauger

Average Size: 13 to 16 inches, 1 to 2 pounds

Records: state—12 pounds, 13 ounces, Alum Creek Lake, Delaware County, 2002; North American—15 pounds, 10 ounces, Fort Peck Reservoir, Montana, 1995

Notes: Saugeyes are produced in hatcheries using Walleye eggs and Sauger sperm. Saugeyes are intermediate between Walleyes and Saugers in both appearance and behavior. They tolerate warm water and turbidity (cloudiness) better than Walleyes and establish well in both lakes and streams. In size they average bigger than Saugers but smaller than Walleyes. Unlike many other hybrids they are fertile and can back-cross with either Walleye or Sauger producing fish with many genetic problems. Saugeyes are increasingly popular for stocking in watersheds unsuitable for Walleyes.

Description: long, round body; dark silver or golden to dark olive brown in color; spines in both first dorsal and anal fin; sharp canine teeth; dark spot at base of the three last spines of the dorsal fin; white spot on bottom lobe of tail

Similar Species: Sauger (pg. 86), Saugeye (pg. 88)

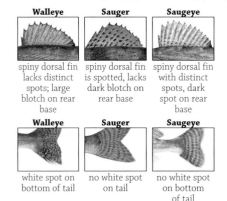

Walleye	Sauger	Saugeye
spiny dorsal fin lacks distinct spots; large blotch on rear base	spiny dorsal fin is spotted, lacks dark blotch on rear base	spiny dorsal fin with distinct spots, dark spot on rear base

Walleye	Sauger	Saugeye
white spot on bottom of tail	no white spot on tail	no white spot on bottom of tail

WALLEYE
Sander vitreus

Other Names: marble-eyes, walleyed pike, jack, jackfish, Susquehanna salmon

Habitat: lakes and streams, abundant in very large lakes

Range: originally the northern states and Canada, now widely stocked throughout the U.S.; native in Lake Erie and Ohio River, now widespread in Ohio's inland waters where it is largely maintained by stocking

Food: mainly small fish, but also insects, crayfish, leeches

Reproduction: spawns in tributary streams or rocky lake shoals when spring water temperatures reach 45–50 degrees F; no parental care

Average Size: 14 to 17 inches, 1 to 3 pounds

Records: state—16 pounds, 3 ounces, Lake Erie, 1999; North American—22 pounds 11, ounces, Greer's Ferry Lake, Arkansas, 1982

Notes: The Walleye is a popular sportfish and the unofficial state fish of Ohio—though Smallmouth Bass fans have argued that point. Not a great fighter, the Walleye is a dogged opponent and fine eating fish. A reflective layer of pigment in the eye allows Walleyes to see in low-light conditions, thus they are most active under cloudy skies, at dusk and dawn and through the night. The Blue Pike, a subspecies (*S. vitreum glaucum*) of the Walleye, was once common in Lake Erie but is now thought to be extinct.

Description: 6 to 9 olive-green vertical bars on a yellow-brown background; two separate dorsal fins—the front all spines, the back soft rays; lower fins tinged yellow or orange brighter in breeding males

Similar Species: Trout-perch (pg. 176), Walleye (pg. 90)

Yellow Perch	Trout-perch	Yellow Perch	Walleye
no adipose fin	adipose fin	lacks prominent white spot on tail	white spot on bottom of tail

YELLOW PERCH

Perca flavescens

Other Names: ringed, striped, jack perch

Habitat: lakes and streams, preferring clear, open water

Range: widely introduced throughout southern Canada and northern U. S.; in Ohio, common in Lake Erie and a few other scattered lakes

Food: prefers minnows, insects, snails, leeches, crayfish

Reproduction: spawns at night in shallow weedy areas when water temperatures reach 45 degrees F; females drapes gelatinous ribbons of eggs over submerged vegetation

Average Size: 8 to 11 inches, 6 to 10 ounces

Records: state—2 pounds, 12 ounces, Lake Erie, 1984; North American—4 pounds, 3 ounces, Bordentown, New Jersey, 1865

Notes: Yellow Perch are very common in Lake Erie and are possibly the most important food and sportfish in that region. Perch congregate in large schools and are active throughout the year, providing endless hours of enjoyment for anglers. Yellow Perch reproduction in the Great Lakes seems to be adversely effected by high Alewife populations. The Yellow Perch population quickly recovers in years that the Alewife population crashes.

Description: olive green to yellow-brown back and sides; wavy yellowish bars on sides; dark teardrop below eye; fins cream to pale yellow; scales on entire cheek and gill covers

Similar Species: Northern Pike (pg. 98)

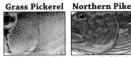

Grass Pickerel   **Northern Pike**

gill cover fully scaled   lower half of gill cover unscaled

Grass Pickerel   **Northern Pike**

vertical bar under eye   no vertical bar under eye

GRASS PICKEREL

Esox americanus vermiculatus

Esocidae

Common Names: mud or little pickerel, grass or mud pike

Habitat: shallow, weedy lakes and sluggish streams

Range: eastern one-third of the United States from the Great Lake basin to Maine and south to Florida (west of Alleghenies) west through Gulf states; northeastern two-thirds of Ohio

Food: small fish, aquatic insects

Reproduction: spawns in early spring just as the ice goes out; adults enter flooded meadows and shallow bays to lay eggs in less than 2 feet of water; adhesive eggs are deposited over shallow, submerged vegetation; eggs are left to hatch with no parental care

Size: 10 to 12 inches, under 1 pound

Records: state—none; North American—1 pound, Dewart Lake, Indiana, 1990

Notes: The Grass Pickerel is the smallest Ohio member of the pike family and inhabits dense vegetation in slow-moving streams and smaller lakes. In large lakes it congregates near stream mouths. Pickerel readily take small lures and minnows and are often discarded by anglers thinking they are baby pike. At times they can be a nuisance for panfish anglers. The relationship between Grass Pickerel and Northern Pike is unclear. In some lakes the species coexist, while in others there is just one or the other.

MUSKELLUNGE

TIGER MUSKIE

Description: torpedo-shaped body; dorsal fin near tail; dark gray-green back; silver to silver green sides; dark vertical bars or blotches on sides (dark markings on light background); tail lobes pointed

Similar Species: Grass Pickerel (pg. 94), Northern Pike (pg. 98), Tiger Muskie

Muskellunge	**Northern Pike**
dark marks on light background	light marks on dark background

Muskellunge	**Northern Pike**
6 or more pores on each side under the jaw	5 or fewer pores on each side under the jaw

Muskellunge	**Grass Pickerel**	**Northern Pike**	**Tiger Muskie**
pointed tail	rounded tail	rounded tail	rounded tail

MUSKELLUNGE
Esox masquinongy

Esocidae

Other Names: muskie, Great Lakes or Ohio Muskellunge

Habitat: waters of large, clear, weedy lakes; medium to large rivers with slow currents and deep pools

Range: the Great Lake basin east to Maine, south through the Ohio River drainage to Tennessee; native throughout Ohio, Tiger Muskellunge stocked in a few large lakes

Food: small fish

Reproduction: spawning takes place in late spring when water temperatures reach 50 to 60 degrees F; eggs are laid in dead vegetation in tributary streams or shallow bays

Average Size: 30 to 42 inches, 10 to 20 pounds

Records: state—55 pounds, 2 ounces, Piedmont Lake, 1972; North American—69 pounds, 11 ounces, Chippewa Flowage, Wisconsin, 1949

Notes: The Muskellunge is the prize of all freshwater game fishing. This big, fast predator prefers large, shallow, clear lakes. Muskies are rare to uncommon over most of their range—typically one fish every two to three acres. They are hard to entice with lures or bait and musky fishermen average over 50 hours to catch a legal fish. Readily hybridized by the state with Northern Pike to produce Tiger Muskellunge. Tiger muskies are also now reared and stocked in some of Ohio's larger lakes.

Description: elongated body with dorsal fin near tail; head long and flattened in front forming a duck-like snout; dark back; light green sides with bean shaped light spots (light markings on dark background)

Similar Species: Grass Pickerel (pg. 94), Muskellunge (pg. 96), Tiger Muskie

Northern Pike	**Muskellunge**	**Tiger Muskie**
light spots on dark background	dark marks on light background	dark marks on light background

Northern Pike	**Muskellunge**	**Northern Pike**	**Muskellunge**
rounded tail	pointed tail	5 or fewer pores on underside of jaw	6 or more pores on each side under the jaw

NORTHERN PIKE

Esox lucius

Other Names: great northern pickerel, jack or jackfish, hammerhandle, snot rocket

Habitat: lakes and slow-moving streams, often associated with vegetation

Range: northern Europe, Asia and North America; native to the Lake Erie drainage, now stocked in the rest of Ohio

Food: small fish, occasionally frogs, crayfish

Reproduction: in early spring as water temperatures reach 34 to 40 degrees F, eggs are laid among shallow vegetation in tributary streams or lake edges; no parental care

Average Size: 18 to 24 inches, 2 to 5 pounds

Records: state—22 pounds, 6 ounces, Lyre Lake, 1988; North American—46 pounds, 2 ounces, Great Sacandaga Lake, New York, 1940

Notes: This large, fast predator is one of the most widespread freshwater fish in the world and a prime sportfish throughout its range. Its long, tube-shaped body and intramuscular bones are adaptations for quick bursts of speed. Pike are sight feeders and hunt by lying in wait, then capturing their prey with a lightning-fast lunge. Many anglers have lost their catch just at the boat when the pike employed this burst of speed to escape. The Tiger Muskie is a Northern Pike-Muskellunge hybrid and is considered a muskie in bag limits.

Description: back is olive, blue-gray to black with worm-like markings; sides bronze to olive with red spots tinged light brown; lower fins are red-orange with a white leading edge; tail squared or slightly forked

Similar Species: Brown Trout (pg. 102), Lake Trout (pg. 104), Rainbow Trout (pg. 106), Splake

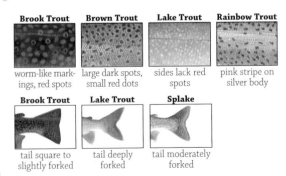

Brook Trout	**Brown Trout**	**Lake Trout**	**Rainbow Trout**
worm-like markings, red spots	large dark spots, small red dots	sides lack red spots	pink stripe on silver body

Brook Trout	**Lake Trout**	**Splake**
tail square to slightly forked	tail deeply forked	tail moderately forked

BROOK TROUT
Salvelinus fontinalis

Salmonidae

Other Names: speckled, squaretail or coaster trout, brookie

Habitat: cool, clear streams and small lakes with sand or gravel bottoms and moderate vegetation; coastal waters of some Great Lakes near tributaries; prefers water temperatures of 50 to 60 degrees F

Range: Great Lakes region north to Labrador, south through the Appalachians to Georgia, introduced into the western U.S., Canada, Europe and South America; native to and now stocked in a few streams in northeast Ohio

Food: insects, small fish

Reproduction: spawns on gravel bars in riffles in late fall when water temperatures reach 40 to 49 degrees F; also spawns in lakes where springs can aerate eggs; female builds 4- to 12-inch- deep nest, then buries fertilized eggs in loose gravel; eggs hatch in 50 to 150 days

Average Size: 8 to 10 inches, 8 ounces

Records: state—none; North American—14 pounds, 8 ounces, Nipigon River, Ontario, 1916

Notes: Due to lack of habitat, this beautiful native fish was originally rare, inhabiting only a few clear, cold streams. Brook Trout still reproduce in a few Ohio streams though most populations are maintained through a limited stocking program. Brook Trout are easily caught fly-fishing and the bright-orange flesh is firm, with a delicate flavor prized by trout fishermen.

101

BROWN TROUT

TIGER TROUT

Description: golden-brown to dark olive back and sides; creamy-white to orange belly; spots on sides, dorsal fin and sometimes upper lobe of tail; few red spots with light halos

Similar Species: Brook Trout (pg. 100), Lake Trout (pg. 104), Rainbow Trout (pg. 106), Tiger Trout

Brown Trout	**Lake Trout**	**Rainbow Trout**
dark spots on brown or olive	white spots on dark background	pink stripe on silvery body

Brown Trout	**Brook Trout**	**Tiger Trout**
lacks worm-like markings on back and sides	worm-like markings on back	worm-like markings on back and sides

102

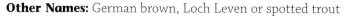

BROWN TROUT

Salmo trutta

Other Names: German brown, Loch Leven or spotted trout

Habitat: open ocean near its spawning streams and clear, cold, gravel-bottomed streams; shallow portions of the Great Lakes

Range: native to Europe from the Mediterranean to Arctic Norway and Siberia; introduced worldwide; in Ohio, Lake Erie and Cold Creek in Erie County and a few other streams

Food: insects, crayfish, small fish

Reproduction: spawns October through December in headwater streams, tributaries and stream mouths when migration is blocked; female fans out saucer-shaped nest that male guards until spawning; female covers eggs

Average Size: 11 to 20 inches, 2 to 6 pounds

Records: state—14 pounds, 10 ounces, Lake Erie, 1995; North American—40 pounds, 4 ounces, Little Red River, Arkansas, 1992

Notes: This European trout was brought to North America in the late 1800s. Brown Trout prefer cold, clear streams but will tolerate much warmer water and some turbidity (cloudiness) better than other trout. A favorite of fly-fishermen around the world, this trout is a secretive, hard-to-catch fish that fights hard and has a fine, delicate flavor. Brown Trout often aggressively feed on cloudy, rainy days and at night. Many states have rules restricting night trout fishing. Brown Trout hybridize with Brook Trout to produce the colorful but sterile Tiger Trout.

103

LAKE TROUT

SPLAKE

Description: dark gray to gray-green on head, back, top fins and tail; white spots on the sides and unpaired fins (light spots on dark background); tail deeply forked; inside of mouth white

Similar Species: Brook Trout (pg. 100), Splake

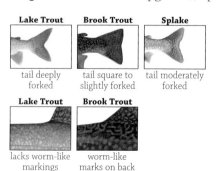

Lake Trout	Brook Trout	Splake
tail deeply forked	tail square to slightly forked	tail moderately forked

Lake Trout	Brook Trout
lacks worm-like markings	worm-like marks on back

LAKE TROUT

Salvelinus namaycush

Other Names: touge, mackinaw, great gray trout, laker

Habitat: cold (less than 65 degrees F), oxygen-rich waters of deep, clear, infertile lakes

Range: Great Lakes north through Canada, east into northeastern U.S., stocked in the Rocky Mountains; native to Lake Erie in Ohio

Food: insects when very young, small fish to maturity

Reproduction: females scatter eggs over rocky lake shoals when water temperatures dip below 50 degrees F in fall

Average Size: 15 to 20 inches, 7 to 10 pounds

Records: state—20 pounds, 8 ounces, Lake Erie, 2000; North American—72 pounds, 4 ounces, Great Bear Lake, N.W.T. Canada, 1995

Notes: The Lake Trout is native to Ohio and has always been an important part of the Lake Erie fishery, prized for both food and sport. The Lake Trout population was decimated in the early 1950s by overfishing and the introduction of the Sea Lamprey. With restocking and aggressive lamprey control, the population has returned to sportfishing levels. Lake Trout are often caught by trolling deep in summer or "surf" fishing in shallower water during the spring and fall. Hybridizes with Brook Trout to produce Splake.

Description: blue-green to brown head and back; silver lower sides with pink to rose stripe; entire body covered with small black spots; adipose fin

Similar Species: Brook Trout (pg. 100), Brown Trout (pg. 102), Pink Salmon (pg. 112)

lacks worm-like markings

worm-like marks on back

pinkish stripe on silvery body

sides lack pinkish stripe

white mouth

dark tongue and jaw tip

Salmonidae

RAINBOW TROUT

Oncorhynchus mykiss

Other Names: steelhead, Pacific, Kamloops or silver trout

Habitat: prefers whitewater in cool streams and coastal regions of large lakes; tolerates smaller cool, clear lakes

Range: Pacific Ocean and coastal streams from Mexico to Alaska and northeast Russia; introduced worldwide; stocked in Lake Erie and other suitable lakes and streams in Ohio

Food: insects, small crustaceans, fish

Reproduction: predominantly spring spawners but some fall spawning varieties exist; female builds nest in well-aerated gravel in both streams and lakes

Average Size: streams—10 to 12 inches, 1 pound; lakes—20 to 22 inches, 2 to 3 pounds

Records: state—20 pounds, 15 ounces, Lake Erie, 1996; North American—(sea-run) 42 pounds, 2 ounces, Bell Island, Alaska, 1970; (inland) 37 pounds, Lake Pend Oreille, Idaho, 1947

Notes: This Pacific trout was first stocked in Ohio in 1884 with fish from Michigan and stocking has continued to the present. The only reproducing populations in Ohio are found in Cold Creek and to a lesser degree Lake Erie. Rainbow Trout caught in Ohio are the results of continuous restocking. Steelhead are Rainbow Trout that migrate from spawning streams into the open ocean or large lakes for part of their life. An exciting sportfishery has been created by introducing steelhead into Lake Erie.

107

Description: iridescent green to blue-green back and upper sides; silver below lateral line; small black spots on back and tail; inside of mouth is dark; breeding males olive brown to purple with pronounced kype (hooked snout)

Similar Species: Coho Salmon (pg. 110), Pink Salmon (pg. 112), Rainbow Trout (pg. 106)

Chinook Salmon

Coho Salmon

Pink Salmon

small spots throughout tail

spots only in top half of tail

eye-sized spots throughout tail

Chinook Salmon

Coho Salmon

Rainbow Trout

inside of mouth is dark

inside of mouth is gray

inside of mouth is white

CHINOOK SALMON

Oncorhynchus tshawytscha

Other Names: king or spring salmon, tyee, quinnat, black mouth

Habitat: open ocean and large, clear, gravel-bottomed rivers; open waters of the Great Lakes and spawning streams

Range: Pacific Ocean north from California to Japan, introduced to the Atlantic coast; in Ohio, Lake Erie and mouths of larger tributary streams

Food: insects, small fish, crustaceans

Reproduction: chinooks in the Great Lakes mature in 3 to 5 years; in September and October they migrate upstream to spawn on gravel bars; eggs hatch the following spring; adults die shortly after spawning

Average Size: 24 to 30 inches, 15 to 20 pounds

Records: state—29 pounds, 8 ounces, Lake Erie, 1989; North American—(inland) 44 pounds, 14 ounces, Lake Michigan, 1994; (sea-run) 97 pounds, 4 ounces, Kenai River, Alaska, 1989

Notes: Largest member of the salmon family, chinooks may reach over 40 pounds in land-locked lakes and much larger in the Pacific. Prior to the 1960s many unsuccessful attempts were made to introduce Chinook Salmon into the Great Lakes region. Since 1965 a stable population of hatchery reared fish has been maintained in Lake Erie, creating one of the most important sportfisheries in the state. A "put-and-take" fish with little or no natural reproduction.

109

Description: dark metallic blue to green back; silver sides and belly; small dark spots on back, sides and upper half of tail; inside of mouth gray; breeding adults gray to green head with red to maroon sides; males develop kype (hooked snout)

Similar Species: Chinook Salmon (pg. 108), Pink Salmon (pg. 112), Rainbow Trout (pg. 106)

Coho Salmon

spots only in top half of tail

Chinook Salmon

small spots throughout tail

Pink Salmon

eye-sized spots throughout tail

Coho Salmon

inside of mouth is gray

Rainbow Trout

inside of mouth is white

COHO SALMON

Oncorhynchus kisutch

Other Names: silver salmon, sea trout, blueback

Habitat: open ocean near spawning streams and clear, gravel-bottomed streams; open Great Lakes waters within 10 miles of shore

Range: Pacific Ocean north from California to Japan, Atlantic coast of U.S., Great Lakes; in Ohio, Lake Erie and mouths of larger tributary streams, especially the Chagrin and Huron rivers

Food: insects, small fish such as Rainbow Smelt and Alewives

Reproduction: spawns in October and November; adults migrate up streams to build nests on gravel bars; parent fish die shortly after spawning

Average Size: 20 inches, 4 to 5 pounds

Records: state—13 pounds, 10 ounces, Huron River, 1982; North American—(sea-run) 31 pounds, Cowichan Bay, B.C., Canada, 1947; (inland) 33 pounds, 4 ounces, Salmon River, New York, 1989

Notes: This Pacific salmon was first stocked in Lake Erie in 1876 and many attempts to establish cohos were made for the next 100 years. Coho still do not reproduce well in any of the Great Lakes and the populations are maintained by stocking. Coho Salmon migrate up streams to spawn in the fall after spending two years in the open lake. A very strong fighter and excellent table fare, it is an important sportfish in Ohio.

Description: steel blue to blue-green back with silver sides; dark spots on back and tail, some as large as eye; breeding males form a large hump in front of dorsal fins and a hooked upper jaw (kype); both sexes are pink during spawning

Similar Species: Brown Trout (pg. 102), Chinook Salmon (pg. 108), Coho Salmon (pg. 110), Rainbow Trout (pg. 106)

Pink Salmon	Chinook Salmon	Coho Salmon
eye-sized spots throughout tail	small spots throughout tail	spots only in top half of tail

Pink Salmon	Brown Trout	Coho Salmon	Rainbow Trout
dark tongue and jaw tip	inside of mouth is white	inside of mouth is gray	inside of mouth is white

PINK SALMON
Oncorhynchus gorbuscha

Other Names: autumn or humpback salmon, humpy

Habitat: coastal Pacific Ocean and open water of the Great Lakes, spawns in clear streams

Range: coastal Pacific Ocean from northern California to Alaska, Great Lakes; Lake Erie in Ohio

Food: small fish, crustaceans

Reproduction: spawns in tributary streams usually at two years of age; female builds nest on gravel bar, then covers fertilized eggs; adults die after spawning

Average Size: 17 to 19 inches, 1 to 2 pounds

Records: state—none; North American—12 pounds, 9 ounces, Moose and Kenai rivers, Alaska, 1974

Notes: This Pacific salmon was unintentionally released into Lake Superior's Thunder Bay in 1956 and has spread throughout the Great Lakes, first spawning in Ohio in the late 1970s. Pink Salmon spend two to three years in the open lake then move into streams to spawn and die. Pink Salmon are infrequently seen in Ohio spawning streams but a few are caught by anglers each year. They are not considered good table fare; the flesh deteriorates rapidly and must be quickly put on ice.

Description: silver with faint pink or purple tinge; dark back; light-colored tail; small mouth; long body but deeper than Rainbow Smelt

Similar Species: Lake Whitefish (pg. 116), Mooneye (pg. 78), Rainbow Smelt (pg. 122)

| | **Lake** | | |
| **Cisco** | **Whitefish** | **Cisco** | **Mooneye** |

jaws equal length or slight underbite / snout protrudes beyond lower jaw   adipose fin / lacks adipose fin

Cisco   **Rainbow Smelt**

deep body (also inconspicuous teeth) / slim profile (also prominent teeth)

CISCO

Coregonus artedi

Other Names: shallow water, common or Great Lakes cisco, lake herring, tullibee

Habitat: shoal waters of the Great Lakes and nutrient-poor inland lakes with oxygen-rich depths that remain cool during summer

Range: northeastern U.S., Great Lakes and Canada; Lake Erie in Ohio

Food: plankton, small crustaceans, aquatic insects

Reproduction: spawns in November and December when water temperatures reach the lower 30s F; eggs are deposited over clean bottoms in 3 to 8 feet of water

Average Size: 10 to 12 inches, 1 pound

Records: state—none; North American—7 pounds, 4 ounces, Cedar Lake, Manitoba, 1986

Notes: Ciscoes were once the most productive commercial fish in the Great Lakes. With overfishing, introduced competitors and pollution, the population collapsed. Often, fish marketed as smoked whitefish are imported Ciscoes. Those in Lake Erie can take several forms ranging from torpedo shaped to deep-bodied fish. Ciscoes can be caught through the ice in winter and were once very popular with Lake Erie anglers (one Ohio fisherman reported catching 300 pounds in a day). They can also provide great sport for the fly-fisherman in summer.

Description: silver with a dark brown to olive back and tail; snout protrudes past lower jaw; small mouth; two small flaps between the openings of each nostril

Similar Species: Cisco (pg. 114), Mooneye (pg. 78), Rainbow Smelt (pg. 122)

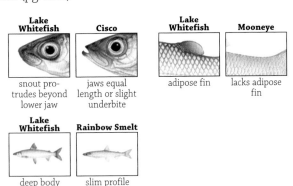

Lake Whitefish	Cisco	Lake Whitefish	Mooneye
snout protrudes beyond lower jaw	jaws equal length or slight underbite	adipose fin	lacks adipose fin

Lake Whitefish	Rainbow Smelt
deep body	slim profile

LAKE WHITEFISH
Coregonus clupeaformis

Other Names: eastern, common or Great Lakes whitefish, Otsego bass, Sault whitefish

Habitat: large, deep, clean inland lakes with oxygen-rich depths during summer; shallow areas of the Great Lakes

Range: from the Great Lakes north across North America; Lake Erie in Ohio

Food: zooplankton, insects, small fish

Reproduction: spawns on gravel bars in late fall when water temperatures reach the low 30s F; occasionally ascends streams to spawn

Average Size: 18 inches, 3 to 4 pounds

Records: state—none; North American—15 pounds, 6 ounces, Clear Lake, Ontario, 1983

Notes: The largest whitefish in North America and an important food fish from presettlement times to the present. With the control of lampreys and the smelt population collapse, the commercial whitefish harvest has rebounded in the upper Great Lakes. In Ohio it is a treat to get fresh whitefish in restaurants along Lake Erie. With Walleye and Lake Trout, Lake Whitefish are considered by many to be the finest food fish from northern waters. Just before the ice forms in the fall, Lake Whitefish move shallow to spawn and were traditionally netted at this time.

Description: slate-gray to blotchy olive-brown back; dark brown streaks on fins; large mouth; eyes set almost on top of head; large, wing-like pectoral fins; no scales

Similar Species: Round Goby (pg. 48)

Mottled Sculpin

lacks scales

Round Goby

scales present

MOTTLED SCULPIN
Cottus bairdii

Other Names: common sculpin, muddler, gudgeon

Habitat: bottom-dwellers of cool, swift, hard-bottom streams or wave-swept lakeshores with rock or vegetation for cover

Range: eastern U.S. through Canada to Hudson Bay and the Rocky Mountains; native to central Ohio and Lake Erie

Food: aquatic invertebrates, fish eggs, small fish

Reproduction: spawns in late spring when water temperatures reach 63 to 73 degrees F; male builds nest under ledge, log or stream bank then entices female with an elaborate courtship; females turn upside down to deposit eggs on "roof" of nest; male attends nest through hatching

Average Size: 4 to 5 inches

Records: none

Notes: A fish of cool, fast streams, the sculpin inhabits the same waters as Rainbow and Brown Trout, though it can tolerate somewhat warmer water than trout. Sculpins were once common in the headwater streams of glaciated Ohio, but now with the depletion of these springs, stream sculpins have become rare. They are scary looking but perfectly harmless and are forage for many top predators. Several species of deepwater sculpins native to the Great Lakes are now extinct, or nearly so, in Ohio.

119

Description: long, thin body; sides bright silver to silver-green with conspicuous light stripe; upturned mouth; 2 dorsal fins; tail deeply forked and pointed

Similar Species: Blackstripe Topminnow (pg. 174), Common Shiner (pg. 74), Rainbow Smelt (pg. 122)

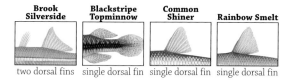

Brook Silverside	Blackstripe Topminnow	Common Shiner	Rainbow Smelt
two dorsal fins	single dorsal fin	single dorsal fin	single dorsal fin

BROOK SILVERSIDE

Atherinidae

Labidesthes sicculus

Other Names: northern silverside, skipjack, friar

Habitat: surface of clear lakes, slack water of large streams

Range: Great Lake states south through central U.S. to Gulf states; uncommon, but found throughout Ohio

Food: aquatic and flying insects, spiders

Reproduction: spawns in late spring and early summer; eggs are laid in sticky strings that are attached to vegetation

Average Size: 3 to 4 inches

Records: none

Notes: The silverside is in a large family of fish that is mostly tropical and subtropical and primarily marine. It is a flashy fish that is often seen cruising near the surface in small schools. Its upturned mouth is an adaptation to surface feeding, and it's not uncommon to see Brook Silverside leap from the water, flying fish style, in pursuit of prey. Silversides have short life spans lasting only 15 months. These sight feeders seem to become listless and feed less when water becomes turbid (cloudy).

Description: dark green back; silver to violet-blue sides; large mouth with prominent teeth; large eye; deeply forked tail; adipose fin

Similar Species: Alewife (pg. 50), Cisco (pg. 114), Common Shiner (pg. 74), Lake Whitefish (pg. 116)

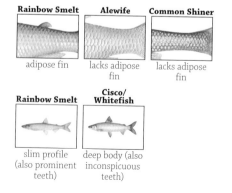

Rainbow Smelt	Alewife	Common Shiner
adipose fin	lacks adipose fin	lacks adipose fin

Rainbow Smelt	Cisco/ Whitefish
slim profile (also prominent teeth)	deep body (also inconspicuous teeth)

RAINBOW SMELT

Osmerus mordax

Other Names: ice or frost fish, lake herring, leefish

Habitat: open ocean and cool, medium depths of large lakes; tributary streams during spawn

Range: Pacific, Atlantic and Arctic oceans, landlocked in southeast Canada and northeast U.S.; Lake Erie in Ohio

Food: crustaceans, insect larvae, small fish

Reproduction: spawn in May at night in the first mile of tributary streams (over bars in open ocean); a single female lays up to 50,000 eggs that are fertilized by several males waiting downstream; eggs sink, attach to the bottom on short pedestals

Average Size: 8 to 10 inches

Records: none

Notes: Smelt are marine fish that enter freshwater to spawn. A few northeastern lakes contain native populations. In 1912 fish from Maine were introduced into Michigan lakes as food for salmon. Smelt escaped into Lake Michigan and spread to the rest of the Great Lakes (except Ontario, where there is a native population). This small fish was soon making spectacular spawning runs in tributary streams. The Great Lakes' smelt population crashed in the 1980s and has not recovered. Smelt are a good forage fish for large predators but consume sportfish fry and compete with them for food. Anglers dip net these tasty fish during the spawning run or fish them through the ice.

Description: mottled brown back and sides; torpedo-shaped body with very narrow caudal peduncle (area just before tail); front portion of dorsal fin has 4 to 6 short, separated spines; pelvic fin abdominal, reduced to single fin; small, sharp teeth

Similar Species: distinguishable from other Ohio fish by 4 to 6 dorsal spines not connected by a membrane

BROOK STICKLEBACK

Culaea inconstans

Gasterosteidae

Other Names: common or many-spined stickleback, spiny minnow

Habitat: shallows of clear, cool streams and lakes

Range: Kansas through northern U.S. and Canada; native to streams in glaciated Ohio, now restricted to trout streams

Food: small aquatic animals

Reproduction: male builds a golf-ball-size globular nest of sticks and algae that hangs on submerged vegetation; female enters nest to deposit eggs then departs, often plowing a hole in the side; male repairs nest and viciously guards the eggs until they hatch; male may build a second nest and move the eggs

Average Size: 2 to 4 inches

Records: none

Notes: Most members of the stickleback family are marine fish but some are equally at home in fresh- or saltwater. There are four sticklebacks in the U.S., only one in Ohio. Highly tolerant of alkaline and acid conditions but not turbidity (cloudiness) these little fish are becoming rare over much of their range as water conditions deteriorate. The Brook Stickleback is now restricted to a few tributaries of Lake Erie in Ohio. These pugnacious little predators make fun aquarium fish, and will readily build and defend nests in captivity, though they may require live food when first captured (mosquito larvae work well).

Description: dark gray to black back; slate-gray to gray-green sides; bony plates on skin; tail shark-like, with upper lobe longer than lower; blunt snout with four barbels; spiracles (openings between eye and corner of gill)

Similar Species: Shovelnose Sturgeon (pg. 128)

Lake Sturgeon	**Shovelnose Sturgeon**
spiracle between eye and gill	lacks spiracles

LAKE STURGEON

Acipenseridae

Acipenser fulvescens

Other Names: rock, stone, red, black or smoothback sturgeon

Habitat: quiet waters in large rivers and lakes

Range: Hudson Bay, Great Lakes, Mississippi and Missouri drainages southeast to Alabama; in Ohio, native to Lake Erie and the Ohio River and its large tributaries

Food: snails, clams, crayfish, aquatic insects

Reproduction: spawns from April through June in lake shallows and tributary streams; up to 1 million eggs are laid and fertilized a few at a time

Average Size: 3 to 5 feet, 5 to 40 pounds

Records: state—none; North American—168 pounds, Nattawasaga Lake, Ontario, 1982

Notes: Sturgeons are the most primitive bony fish alive today, with relatives dating back more than 350 million years. They are bottom feeders that require clear, clean, deep lakes or river pools. They mature slowly, and do not spawn until 10 to 20 years of age. Lake Sturgeon more than 300 pounds in weight and 100 years old have been reported from southern Canada. Once common, they are now very rare in the Ohio and Scioto rivers. The largest Ohio population is in Lake Erie. Not thought of as a sportfish in Ohio, they are pursued by anglers in other Great Lakes states such as Minnesota and Wisconsin.

Description: coppery tan to light brown back and sides; long flat snout; bony plates instead of scales; shark-like tail, long upper lobe ending in long filament

Similar Species: Lake Sturgeon (pg. 126)

Shovelnose Sturgeon **Lake Sturgeon**

lacks spiracles   spiracle between eye and gill

SHOVELNOSE STURGEON

Acipenseridae

Scaphirhynchus platorynchus

Other Names: hackleback, sand sturgeon, switchtail

Habitat: open, flowing channels of rivers and large streams, typically with sand or gravel bottoms

Range: Hudson Bay south through central U.S., west to New Mexico east to Kentucky; in Ohio, native to the Ohio River

Food: clams, snails, crayfish, insects

Reproduction: spawns in spring when water temperatures reach 65 to 70 degrees F; adults migrate upriver to dams or into small tributaries; eggs are deposited in swift current over gravel bars; spawns below dams when necessary

Average Size: 2 feet, 3 pounds

Records: state—none; North American—8 pounds, 5 ounces, Rock River, Illinois, 1998

Notes: The Shovelnose Sturgeon is the smallest sturgeon in North America. This prehistoric-looking fish has cartilage instead of bones and hard plates instead of scales. It is restricted to the Ohio River and congregates below the dams to spawn. The Shovelnose Sturgeon is listed as an endangered species in Ohio.

Description: olive-brown to bronze back; dull olive-green sides fading to white belly; blunt snout; rounded head; long dorsal fin; large forward-facing mouth with thin lips; upper lip almost level with eye

Similar Species: Black Buffalo (pg. 132), Common Carp (pg. 62)

mouth lacks barbels, upper lip almost level with eye

Black Buffalo

upper lip well below eye

Common Carp

barbels below mouth, upper lip well below eye

BIGMOUTH BUFFALO

Ictiobus cyprinellus

Other Names: baldpate, blue router, mongrel, prairie or round buffalo, router

Habitat: soft-bottomed shallows of large lakes, sloughs and oxbows; slow-flowing rivers and streams

Range: Saskatchewan to Lake Erie south through the Mississippi River drainage to the Gulf of Mexico; in Ohio, the Ohio and Scioto rivers, and the Sandusky River and bay in the Lake Erie drainage

Food: small mollusks, aquatic insect larvae, zooplankton

Reproduction: spawns in early spring in clear, shallow water in flooded fields and marshes when water temperatures reach the low 60s F; young quickly return to main lake or river when water recedes

Average Size: 18 to 20 inches, 10 to 12 pounds

Records: state—(unspecific buffalo) 46 pounds, Hover Reservoir, 1999; North American—73 pounds, 1 ounce, Lake Koshkonong, Wisconsin, 2004

Notes: This large, schooling fish is a filter feeder and commercially harvested with nets in the Ohio River but not often taken on hook and line. Bigmouth Buffalo can tolerate low oxygen levels, high water temperatures and some turbidity (cloudiness) but prefer to forage in clean, clear water. This big, strong fighter is good to eat and would be a world-class sportfish if it would more readily take a hook.

Description: slate-green to dark gray back; sides have a blue-bronze sheen; deep body with sloping back supporting a long dorsal fin; upper lip well below eye

Similar Species: Bigmouth Buffalo (pg. 130), Common Carp (pg. 62)

Black Buffalo	Bigmouth Buffalo	Common Carp
mouth lacks barbels; upper lip well below eye	upper lip almost level with eye	barbels below mouth

BLACK BUFFALO

Ictiobus niger

Other Names: buoy tender, current or deep-water buffalo

Habitat: deep, fast water of large streams; deep sloughs, backwaters and impoundments

Range: lower Great Lakes and southern Mississippi River drainage west to South Dakota, south to New Mexico and Louisiana; in Ohio, the Ohio and Scioto rivers

Food: aquatic insects, crustaceans, algae

Reproduction: spawns in April and May when water reaches the low 60s F; adults move up tributaries to lay eggs in flooded sloughs and marshes

Average Size: 15 to 20 inches, 10 to 12 pounds

Records: state—(unspecific buffalo) 46 pounds, Hover Reservoir, 1999; North American—63 pounds, 6 ounces, Mississippi River, Iowa, 1999

Notes: The Black Buffalo is a southern species that inhabits the deep, strong currents of large rivers. Large numbers sometimes gather near buoys at the edge of channels. They were once very common in the Ohio and Scioto rivers and an important part of the commercial harvest. They are much less common now and seem to be affected by the invasion of the Asian carps. Seldom caught by anglers, Black Buffalo can be locally abundant and when hooked, put up a tremendous fight in fast water.

Description: bright silver back and sides, often with yellow tinge; fins clear; deep body with round blunt head; leading edge of dorsal fin extends into a large, arching "quill"

Similar Species: Common Carp (pg. 62)

Quillback   **Common Carp**

mouth lacks   barbels below
barbels   mouth

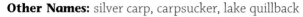

Catostomidae

QUILLBACK
Carpiodes cyprinus

Other Names: silver carp, carpsucker, lake quillback

Habitat: slow-flowing streams and rivers; backwaters and lakes, particularly areas with soft bottoms

Range: south-central Canada through the Great Lakes to the eastern U.S., south through the Mississippi drainage to the gulf; in Ohio, carpsuckers are widespread including Lake Erie

Food: insects, plant matter, decaying bottom material

Reproduction: spawns in late spring through early summer in tributaries or lake shallows; eggs are deposited in open areas over sand or mud

Average Size: 12 to 14 inches, 1 to 3 pounds

Records: state—none; North American—8 pounds, 13 ounces, Lake Winnebago, 2003

Notes: In North America there are four fish known as carp-suckers. The Quillback is one of the three found in Ohio; all are difficult to tell apart. Quillbacks prefer medium to large rivers and lakes, and even through they are rare in one stream, they can be very common in the next. They are schooling fish that filter feed along the bottom. Not sought by anglers but readily take wet flies and can be very sporting when caught on light tackle. The flesh is white and very flavorful.

Description: back brassy-green to gold; bronze to golden-green sides; off-white belly; dorsal and tail slate gray; lower fins yellowish orange to dull red; blunt nose and ventrally placed sucker mouths; sickle-shaped dorsal fin

Similar Species: Northern Hog Sucker (pg. 138), White Sucker (pg. 140)

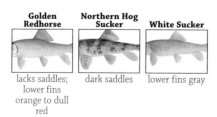

Golden Redhorse — lacks saddles; lower fins orange to dull red

Northern Hog Sucker — dark saddles

White Sucker — lower fins gray

GOLDEN REDHORSE

Moxostoma erythrurum

Catostomidae

Other Names: golden sucker, golden or smallheaded mullet

Habitat: clean streams and rivers with hard bottoms; rarely clear lakes with strong tributary streams

Range: Great Lakes states to New England south to the Gulf; in Ohio, Lake Erie and most large to medium-size streams

Food: aquatic insects, small crustaceans, plant debris

Reproduction: spawns from late May to June when water temperatures reach the low 60s F; adults migrate into small tributary streams to lay eggs on shallow gravel bars in the current near deep pools

Average Size: 18 to 24 inches, 2 to 5 pounds

Records: state—none; North American—3 pounds, 15 ounces, Root River, Minnesota, 2007

Notes: There are seven redhorses in Ohio ranging from 2 to 10 pounds. The Golden is one of the most common and widespread. All are "sucker-type fish" rather similar in appearance and hard to tell apart. They are clean-water fish very susceptible to increased turbidity (cloudiness) and pollutants. Redhorses are more commonly found in streams but do inhabit a few lakes. They may all look alike but each is a separate species and occupies its own niche in Ohio waters. Not of sporting importance but Redhorses are a fairly common catch of river anglers. They fight well on light tackle and though bony have a good flavor when smoked.

137

Description: back dark olive brown fading to yellow-brown blotches on sides; 4 to 5 irregular dark saddles; elongated body almost round in cross section; large head that is concave between the eyes; lower fins are dull red

Similar Species: Golden Redhorse (pg. 136), White Sucker (pg. 140)

Northern Hog Sucker	Golden Redhorse	Northern Hog Sucker	White Sucker
dark saddles	sides lack saddles	head concave between eyes	head flat to raised between eyes

Catostomidae

NORTHERN HOG SUCKER

Hypentelium nigricans

Other Names: hog molly, hammerhead, riffle or bigheaded sucker, crawl-a-bottom

Habitat: riffles and tailwaters of clear streams with hard bottoms; found in a few lakes near the mouths of tributary streams

Range: central and eastern Canada and the U.S. south to Alabama, west to Oklahoma; common in clear Ohio streams and a few lakes; uncommon in Lake Erie

Food: small crustaceans, aquatic insects

Reproduction: spawns in April and May when water reaches low 60s F; males gather in riffles or downstream ends of pools; females enter spawning areas just long enough to shed eggs, which are fertilized by several males; no parental care

Average Size: 10 to 12 inches, 1 pound

Records: state—none; North American—1 pound, 12 ounces, Fox River, Wisconsin, 2004

Notes: Northern Hog Suckers are clean-water fish well adapted to feeding in moving water. They use their elongated shape and concave head to hold their place in riffles while turning over stones to find food. It is common for other fish to follow hog suckers to feed on what is stirred up. Hog suckers are not of much interest to anglers but are sometimes caught by trout fishermen working the edge of fast water.

Description: back olive to brownish; sides gray to silver; belly off-white; dorsal and tail fin slate; lower fins tinged orange; snout barely extends beyond upper lip; breeding males develop black or purple stripe that fades in minutes when the fish is handled

Similar Species: Golden Redhorse (pg. 136), Northern Hog Sucker (pg. 138)

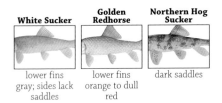

White Sucker	Golden Redhorse	Northern Hog Sucker
lower fins gray; sides lack saddles	lower fins orange to dull red	dark saddles

WHITE SUCKER

Catostomus commersoni

Other Names: common, coarse-scaled or eastern sucker, bay fish, black mullet

Habitat: clear to turbid (cloudy) streams, rivers and lakes

Range: Canada through central and eastern U.S. south to a line from New Mexico to South Carolina; common in waters throughout Ohio

Food: insects, crustaceans, plant material

Reproduction: in early spring when water reaches high 50s to low 60s F, adults spawn in tributary riffles over gravel or coarse sand; in lakes, eggs are deposited over shallow gravel or rocks along wave-swept shorelines

Average Size: 12 to 18 inches, 1 to 3 pounds

Records: state—(unspecific sucker) 9 pounds, 4 ounces, Leesville Lake, 1977 (not registered as a North American record); North American—7 pounds, 4 ounces, Big Round Lake, Wisconsin, 1978

Notes: The White Sucker is one of the most common fish in Ohio and one of the most important. Highly productive, it provides a large source of forage for game fish and is a mainstay in the bait industry. White Suckers are not the great consumers of trout eggs they were once thought to be, but may compete with trout fry for food when first hatched. White Suckers are most often fished during the spring spawning run. The flesh is firm and good tasting.

141

Description: dark green back; greenish sides often with dark lateral band; large forward-facing mouth; lower jaw extends to rear margin of eye

Similar Species: Smallmouth Bass (pg. 144), Spotted Bass (pg. 146)

Largemouth Bass	Smallmouth Bass	Spotted Bass
mouth extends well beyond non-red eye	mouth does not extend beyond red eye	jaw does not extend well beyond eye

LARGEMOUTH BASS

Centrarchidae

Micropterus salmoides

Other Names: black, bayou, green or slough bass, green trout

Habitat: shallow, fertile, weedy lakes and river backwaters; weedy bays of large lakes

Range: southern Canada through U.S. into Mexico, extensively introduced worldwide; common throughout Ohio

Food: small fish, frogs, crayfish, insects

Reproduction: spawning takes place in May and June when water temperatures reach 60 degrees F; male builds nest in weedbed less than 6 feet deep; male fans and guards the nest until the "brood swarm" disperses

Average Size: 12 to 20 inches, 1 to 5 pounds

Records: state—13 pounds, 2 ounces, private pond, 1976; North American—22 pounds, 4 ounces, Montgomery Lake, Georgia, 1932

Notes: The Largemouth Bass is the most sought-after game fish in North America. These denizens of the weedbeds are voracious carnivores and eat anything that is alive and will fit into their mouth. Largemouths are native to most of Ohio and by the early 1900s were stocked in any water that would sustain them. Largemouth Bass run 1 to 2 pounds with 6- and 7-pounders not uncommon in Ohio. They are very tasty when small and from clean water, but tend to be slightly muddy flavored when taken from silty water.

Description: back and sides mottled dark green to bronze or pale gold, often with dark vertical bands; white belly; stout body; large, forward-facing mouth; red eye

Similar Species: Largemouth Bass (pg. 142), Spotted Bass (pg. 146)

Smallmouth Bass

Largemouth Bass

Smallmouth Bass

Spotted Bass

mouth does not extend beyond red eye

mouth extends well beyond non-red eye

vertical bars on sides

lateral stripe on sides

SMALLMOUTH BASS

Micropterus dolomieui

Other Names: bronzeback, redeye bass, redeye, white or mountain trout

Habitat: clear, swift-flowing streams and rivers; clear lakes with gravel or rocky shorelines

Range: native in eastern U.S., extensively introduced world-wide; statewide in Ohio

Food: insect, small fish, crayfish

Reproduction: male builds nest in 3 to 10 feet of water (may be up to 20 feet in the clear waters of Lake Erie) on open gravel beds when water temperatures reach mid- to high 60s F; nest is often near logs or boulders; male aggressively guard the nest and young until fry disperse

Average Size: 12 to 20 inches, 1 to 4 pounds

Records: state—9 pounds, 8 ounces, Lake Erie, 1993; North American—11 pounds, 15 ounces, Dale Hollow Lake, Tennessee, 1955

Notes: Smallmouth Bass are world-class game fish noted for their strong fights and high jumps. Native to Ohio, mainly the Lake Erie drainage, they were netted commercially until the early 1900s. Overfishing, damming streams and siltation have greatly reduced smallmouth populations in Ohio; still, Lake Erie is a premiere fishery. Avoiding weed-beds, Smallmouth Bass prefer deeper, more open water than Largemouth Bass.

Description: dark green back fading to lighter green sides; diamond-shaped blotches form dark stripe on side; dark spots above stripe; light spots on base of each scale below stripe; dark lines extend from redish eye

Similar Species: Largemouth Bass (pg. 142), Smallmouth Bass (pg. 144)

Spotted Bass / **Largemouth Bass**

mouth does not extend beyond the eye / mouth extends beyond non-red eye

Spotted Bass

lateral stripe on sides

Smallmouth Bass

vertical bars on sides

SPOTTED BASS

Micropterus punctulatus

Other Names: Kentucky, speckled or yellow bass, spot

Habitat: deeper silted pools in sluggish, medium to large streams; larger lakes and reservoirs

Range: the Ohio and Mississippi drainage in the southern U.S. from Florida to Texas; the Ohio River drainage and its larger tributaries in southern Ohio

Food: small fish, crayfish

Reproduction: male builds nest in open gravel beds 3 to 4 feet deep from May to June when water temperatures reach mid- to high 60s F; male aggressively guards the nest and young

Average Size: 8 to 18 inches, 8 ounces to 2 pounds

Records: state—5 pounds, 4 ounces, White Lake, 1976; North American—10 pounds, 4 ounces, Pine Flat Lake, California, 2001

Notes: This bass is primarily a stream fish but has done well in large impoundments. Spotted Bass are intermediate between Largemouth and Smallmouth Bass in habits. Smallmouths prefer steam riffles, largemouths the edges of weedbeds and spots favor the slower, deep pools. In reservoirs they seek deeper water than Smallmouth Bass.

Description: black to olive back; silver sides with dark green to black blotches; back more arched and depression above eye more pronounced than White Crappie

Similar Species: White Crappie (pg. 150)

Black Crappie	**White Crappie**
usually 7 to 8 spines in dorsal fin	usually 5 to 6 spines in dorsal fin

Black Crappie	**White Crappie**
dorsal fin length equal to distance from dorsal to eye	dorsal fin shorter than distance from eye to dorsal

BLACK CRAPPIE

Pomoxis nigromaculatus

Other Names: speck, speckled perch, papermouth

Habitat: quiet, clear water of streams and mid-sized lakes; often associated with vegetation but may roam deep, open basins and flats, particularly during winter

Range: southern Manitoba through Atlantic and south-eastern states, introduced but not common in the West; common throughout Ohio

Food: small fish, aquatic insects, zooplankton

Reproduction: spawns in shallow weedbeds from May to June when water temperatures reach the high 50s F; male builds circular nest in fine gravel or sand, then guards eggs and young until fry begin feeding

Average Size: 7 to 12 inches, 5 ounces to 1 pound

Records: state—4 pounds, 8 ounces, private pond, 1981; North American—6 pounds, Westwego Canal, Louisiana, 1969

Notes: The Black Crappie is the most widespread crappie in Ohio and is found in most lakes that have clear water and good weed growth. Seldom found in moving water. They are the most popular Ohio panfish in all seasons, feeding actively in both winter and summer. Black Crappies are sought for their sweet-tasting white fillets, not their fighting ability. They nest in colonies and often gather in large feeding schools. Black Crappies require clearer water and more vegetation than White Crappies.

149

Description: greenish back; silvery green to white sides with 7 to 9 dark vertical bars; the only sunfish with six spines in both dorsal and anal fin

Similar Species: Black Crappie (pg. 148)

White Crappie

Black Crappie

usually 5 to 6 spines in dorsal fin

usually 7 to 8 spines in dorsal fin

White Crappie

Black Crappie

dorsal fin shorter than distance from eye to dorsal

dorsal fin length equal to distance from dorsal to eye

WHITE CRAPPIE

Pomoxis annularis

Other Names: silver, pale or ringed crappie, papermouth

Habitat: slightly silty streams and mid-size lakes; prefers less vegetation than Black Crappie

Range: North Dakota south and east to the Gulf and Atlantic, except peninsular Florida; common throughout Ohio

Food: aquatic insects, small fish, plankton

Reproduction: spawns on firm sand or gravel when water temperature approaches 60 degrees F; male builds a shallow, round nest, guards eggs and young after spawning

Average Size: 8 to 10 inches, 5 ounces to 1 pound

Records: state—3 pounds, 14 ounces, private pond, 1995; North American—5 pounds, 3 ounces, Enid Dam, Mississippi, 1957

Notes: White Crappies, the southern cousins to Black Crappies, are native to Ohio and are now common throughout the state. They prefer deeper, less weedy, and more turbid (cloudy) water than Black Crappies. Due to their acceptance of turbid water there is some indication of a positive relationship between Common Carp and White Crappie. Black and White Crappies can be found in mixed schools in winter and occasionally hybridize. Both actively feed during winter and at night.

Description: dark olive to green on back, blending to silver-gray, copper, orange, purple or brown on sides; 5 to 9 dark vertical bars on sides that fade with age; yellow belly and copper breast; large dark gill spot that extends completely to gill margin; dark spot on rear margin of dorsal fin

Similar Species: Green Sunfish (pg. 154), Pumpkinseed (pg. 160)

Bluegill	Green Sunfish
small mouth	large mouth

Bluegill	Pumpkinseed
dark gill spot	orange crescent

Bluegill	Pumpkinseed
dark spot on dorsal fin	no dark spot

BLUEGILL

Lepomis macrochirus

Centrarchidae

Other Names: bream, sun perch, blue sunfish, copperbelly, strawberry bass

Habitat: medium to large streams and most lakes with weedy bays or shorelines

Range: southern Canada through the southern states into Mexico; common throughout Ohio

Food: aquatic insects, snails, small fish

Reproduction: spawns from late May to early August when water temperatures reach high 60s to low 80s F; male builds nest in shallow, sparse vegetation in colony of up to 50 other nests; male guards nest and fry

Average Size: 6 to 9 inches, 5 to 8 ounces

Records: state—3 pounds, 4 ounces, Salt Fork Reservoir, 1990; North American—4 pounds, 12 ounces, Ketona Lake, Alabama, 1950

Notes: Bluegills are native to the glaciated parts of Ohio and have spread to the entire state. They are a very popular panfish in Ohio and throughout the United States. Bluegills prefer impoundments and are not often found in streams with much current. They have small mouths and feed mostly on insects and small fish. They often feed on the surface and are popular with fly fishermen. Bluegills prefer deep weedbeds at the edge of open water. Many lakes have large populations of hybrid sunfish, crosses between Bluegills and Green or Pumpkinseed.

Description: dark green back; dark olive to bluish sides; yellow or whitish belly; scales flecked with yellow, producing a brassy appearance; dark gill spot has a pale margin

Similar Species: Bluegill (pg. 152), Pumpkinseed (pg. 160), Redear Sunfish (pg. 162)

Green Sunfish	**Bluegill**	**Pumpkinseed**	**Redear Sunfish**
dark gill spot has a pale margin	dark gill spot lacks prominent pale margin	red/orange margin on gill spot	orange margin on gill spot

Green Sunfish	**Bluegill**
large mouth	small mouth

GREEN SUNFISH

Lepomis cyanellus

Other Names: green perch, sand bass

Habitat: warm, weedy, shallow lakes and the backwaters of slow-moving streams

Range: most of the U.S. into Mexico excluding Florida and the Rocky Mountains; found throughout inland Ohio, recorded from Lake Erie but not common

Food: aquatic insects, small crustaceans, fish

Reproduction: male builds nest in less than a foot of weedy water, in temperatures from 60 to 80 degrees F; may produce two broods per year; male guards nest and fans eggs until hatching

Average Size: 4 to 6 inches, less than 8 ounces

Records: state—12 ounces, private pond, 1994; North American—2 pounds, 2 ounces, Stockton Lake, Missouri, 1971

Notes: Green Sunfish are often mistaken for Bluegills but prefer shallower weedbeds. Very tolerant of turbid (cloudy) water and low oxygen levels, it thrives in warm, weedy lakes and backwaters and has become very common in Ohio out-competing other sunfish. Green Sunfish stunt easily, filling some lakes with 3-inch-long breeding fish. Green Sunfish sometimes hybridize with Bluegills and Pumpkinseeds, producing large, aggressive offspring.

Description: dark greenish blue back; sides light green flecked with blue or yellow; belly and chest bright orange to pale yellow; gill flap tapers into long, black finger with red margin

Similar Species: Redear Sunfish (pg. 162)

Northern Longear Sunfish	Redear Sunfish	Northern Longear Sunfish	Redear Sunfish
dark spots on dorsal fin	no spots on dorsal fin	blue-green bands on side of head	solid green to bronze head

NORTHERN LONGEAR SUNFISH

Centrarchidae

Lepomis megalotis

Other Names: Great Lakes longear, blue-and-orange sunfish, red perch

Habitat: clear, moderately weedy, slow-moving shallow streams, and quiet, clear lakes

Range: central states north to Quebec, east to the Appalachian Mountains and as far south as the Gulf of Mexico, introduced into some western states; common throughout Ohio

Food: small insects, crustaceans, fish

Reproduction: male builds and guards nest on shallow gravel bed when water temperatures reach the mid 70s F

Average Size: 3 to 4 inches, 5 ounces

Records: state—4.8 ounces, Big Darby Creek, 2001; North American—1 pound, 12 ounces, Big Round Lake, New Mexico, 1985

Notes: Longears are colorful, secretive little sunfish that prefer clear, slow-moving streams but also inhabit some clean Ohio lakes. This southern species reaches the limits of it range in the southern Great Lakes region. Northern Longear Sunfish are disappearing from many streams due to increased siltation from agriculture. Longears feed on the surface more than other sunfish. There is some hybridization with other sunfish.

Description: blue-green back fading to orange; about 30 orange or red spots on sides of males, brown spots on females; orange pelvic and anal fins; black gill spot with light margin

Similar Species: Pumpkinseed (pg. 160), Redear Sunfish (pg. 162)

Orangespotted Sunfish	**Pumpkinseed**	**Redear Sunfish**
light margin on gill spot	orange or red crescent on gill flap	orange or red crescent on gill

Orangespotted Sunfish	**Redear Sunfish**
rounded pectoral fin	pointed pectoral fin

ORANGESPOTTED SUNFISH
Lepomis humilis

Other Names: orangespot, dwarf sunfish, pygmy sunfish

Habitat: open to moderately weedy pools with soft bottoms

Range: southern Great Lakes through the Mississippi River basin to the Gulf states; abundant in some lakes throughout Ohio

Food: small insects, crustaceans

Reproduction: male builds and guards nest in shallow weedy water when temperatures reach mid 60s F; colonial nesters with 50 or more nests together in a colony

Average Size: 3 to 4 inches, 4 ounces

Records: none

Notes: This brightly colored sunfish is too small to be an important panfish in Ohio. Orangespotted Sunfish were first recorded in Northwest Ohio and have spread across the state. They survive well in silty water and tolerate slight pollution, making them well suited for small lakes in the eroded landscapes of agricultural areas. Orangespotted Sunfish are important as forage for other game fish and may be important for mosquito (where legal) control in some areas. They make beautiful aquarium fish but may require some live food.

Description: back brown to olive fading to light olive; sides speckled with orange-yellow spots, with 7 to 10 vertical bands; black gill spot with light margin and orange crescent

Similar Species: Bluegill (pg. 152), Green Sunfish (pg. 154),

Pumpkinseed	Bluegill	Pumpkinseed	Green Sunfish
orange or red crescent on gill flap	gill spot lacks light margin	long, pointed pectoral fin	rounded pectoral fin

PUMPKINSEED

Lepomis gibbosus

Centrarchidae

Other Names: round or yellow sunfish, punky, sun bass, bream

Habitat: weedy ponds, lakes, reservoirs and slow-moving streams; prefers slightly cooler water than Bluegill

Range: central and eastern North America, introduced in the West; common throughout Ohio

Food: snails, aquatic and terrestrial insects, small fish

Reproduction: spawns from late May to August when water temperatures reach 55 to 63 degrees F; male builds nest among weeds in less than 2 feet of water with sand or gravel bottom; male aggressively guards the nest; may produce multiple broods

Average Size: 6 to 8 inches, 5 to 8 ounces

Records: state—12 ounces, private pond, 2001; North American—2 pounds, 4 ounces, North Saluda River, South Carolina, 1997

Notes: This small, brightly colored sunfish is one of the most beautiful fish native to Ohio. Historically was present in the northern unglaciated part of Ohio, particularly Lake Erie. In the early 1900s it was heavily stocked in southern Ohio and became well established in lakes but not streams. Pumpkinseeds often gather in small schools around docks and submerged deadfalls. Hybridizes with other sunfish and may totally colonize some lakes. Has specialized teeth for feeding on snails.

Description: back and sides bronze to dark green, fading to light green; faint vertical bars; bluish stripes on side of head; gill flap short with dark spot and red margin in males

Similar Species: Northern Longear Sunfish (pg. 156), Pumpkinseed (pg. 160)

Redear Sunfish

solid green to bronze head lacks blue lines

Northern Longear Sunfish

blue-green bands on side of head

Pumpkinseed

wavy blue lines on head

Redear Sunfish

no spots on dorsal fin

Northern Longear Sunfish

dark spots on dorsal fin

REDEAR SUNFISH
Lepomis microlophus

Other Names: shellcracker, stumpknocker, yellow bream

Habitat: congregates around stumps and logs in low to moderate vegetation in large quiet lakes

Range: northern Midwest through southern states, introduced elsewhere; common in Ohio

Food: mainly mollusks

Reproduction: male builds and guard nest in shallow weedy water in May and June when water temperatures reach high 60s F; may produce second brood well into summer

Average size: 8 to 10 inches, 8 ounces to 1 pound

Records: state—3 pounds, 9 ounces, private pond, 1998; North America—5 pounds, 7.5 ounces, Diversion Canal, South Carolina, 1998

Notes: The Redear Sunfish is a large, highly regarded panfish of the South that has been introduced in many northern and western states. Its native range did not extend into Ohio, but this aggressive sunfish was released in several Ohio lakes in the early 1930s. These introductions were very successful and now Redears are common throughout the state and one of the most popular panfish. They are aggressive feeders in summer and though not as active as Bluegills in winter, can be caught through the ice.

Description: brown to olive green back and sides, overall bronze appearance; each scale on sides has a dark spot; red eye; thicker, heavier body than other sunfish; large mouth

Similar Species: Bluegill (pg. 152), Green Sunfish (pg. 154), Warmouth

Rock Bass	**Bluegill**
large mouth extends to eye	small mouth does not extend to eye

Rock Bass	**Warmouth**
lacks red-brown streaks radiating from eye	red-brown streaks radiate from eye

Rock Bass	**Green Sunfish**
6 spines in anal fin	3 spines in anal fin

ROCK BASS
Ambloplites rupestris

Other Names: redeye, goggle eye, rock sunfish

Habitat: vegetation on rocky bottom in clear-water lakes and medium-size streams

Range: southern Canada through central and eastern U. S. to the northern edge of the Gulf States; common throughout Ohio

Food: prefers crayfish, but eats aquatic insects and small fish

Reproduction: spawns when water temperatures reach high 60s to 70s degrees F; male builds nest in coarse gravel in submerged vegetation less than 3 feet deep; male guards eggs and fry

Average Size: 8 to 10 inches, 8 ounces to 1 pound

Records: state—2 pounds, Deer Creek near London, 1932; North American—3 pounds, York River, Ontario, 1974

Notes: A large sunfish native to Ohio and once found in almost every stream. Lake Erie supported a huge population of Rock Bass that were commercially harvested. They were less common in inland lakes. It is plentiful, a good fighter and often caught but not often sought by fishermen. In both lakes and streams, Rock Bass are normally found over a rocky or gravel substrate even when vegetation is present. Frequently found in schools that stay put, not moving from their home territories. Once these schools are located, Rock Bass are easy to catch.

Description: dark gray back; bright silver sides with 7 or 8 indistinct or broken stripes; dorsal fin separated, front part hard spines rear part soft rays

Similar Species: Striped Bass (pg. 170), White Bass (pg. 168), White Perch (pg. 172)

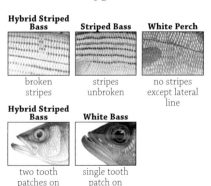

Hybrid Striped Bass	Striped Bass	White Perch
broken stripes	stripes unbroken	no stripes except lateral line

Hybrid Striped Bass	White Bass
two tooth patches on tongue	single tooth patch on tongue

HYBRID STRIPED BASS

Morone saxatilis X Morone chrysops

Moronidae

Other Names: white striper, wiper

Habitat: open water of large lakes and slow moving rivers

Range: stocked in about 40 U.S. states; in Ohio, the Ohio River, Buckeye, Charles Mill, East Fork and Kiser reservoirs and Deer Creek Lake

Food: small fish

Reproduction: hatchery-produced hybrid that is only occasionally fertile

Average Size: 18 to 20 inches, 8 to 10 pounds

Records: state—17 pounds, 11 ounces, Deer Creek Lake, 2001; North American—27 pounds, 5 ounces, Greers Ferry Lake, Arkansas, 1997

Notes: The Hybrid Striped Bass is a hatchery cross between a female (normally) Striped Bass and a male White Bass. They do not reproduce but may back-cross with the parent stock. Ohio now raises large numbers of fingerlings to stock in impoundments too warm to support Striped Bass. This hard fighting, tasty hybrid bass has now become a favorite with anglers in Ohio and across the country. The Hybrid Striped Bass is also becoming an important aquaculture fish supplying fillets for the grocery and restaurant market.

Description: gray-black back; silver sides with 6 to 8 black stripes; front hard-spined portion of dorsal fin separated from soft-rayed rear portion; mouth protrudes beyond snout

Similar Species: Striped Bass (pg. 170), Hybrid Striped Bass (pg. 166), White Perch (pg. 172)

White Bass	**Striped Bass**	**White Bass**	**White Perch**
single spine on gill cover	two spines on gill cover	horizontal black stripes	no stripes except lateral line

White Bass	**Hybrid Striped Bass**	**Striped Bass**
single tooth patch on tongue	two tooth patches on tongue	two tooth patches on tongue

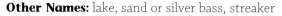

WHITE BASS

Moronidae

Morone chrysops

Other Names: lake, sand or silver bass, streaker

Habitat: large lakes, rivers and impoundments with relatively clear water

Range: Great Lakes to the eastern seaboard, through the Southeast to the Gulf, west to Texas; in Ohio, Lake Erie, a few large impoundments and tributaries of the Ohio River

Food: small fish

Reproduction: spawns in late spring or early summer; eggs spread in open water over gravel beds or rubble 6 to 10 feet deep; some populations migrate to narrow bays or up tributary streams to spawn

Average Size: 18 inches, 8 ounces to 2 pounds

Records: state—4 pounds, gravel pit, 1983; North American—6 pounds, 1 ounces, Saqinaw Bay, Michigan, 1989

Notes: The White Bass is native to Lake Erie and a few streams in the Ohio River drainage and now has been stocked very successfully in other impoundments. In the mid 1800s White Bass were one of the main fish commercially harvested in western Lake Erie. They inhabit large lakes and rivers, where they travel in schools near the surface. White Bass can often be spotted by watching for seagulls feeding on baitfish driven to the surface by schools of bass. The flesh is somewhat soft but has a good flavor.

Description: dark gray back; bright silver sides with 7 or 8 distinct stripes; two tooth patches; dorsal fin separated, front part hard spines, rear part soft rays

Similar Species: Hybrid Striped Bass (pg. 166), White Bass (pg. 168), White Perch (pg. 172)

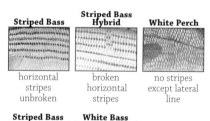

Striped Bass

horizontal stripes unbroken

Striped Bass Hybrid

broken horizontal stripes

White Perch

no stripes except lateral line

Striped Bass

two tooth patches on tongue

White Bass

single tooth patch on tongue

STRIPED BASS
Morone saxatilis

Other Names: striper, streaker, surf bass, rockfish

Habitat: coastal oceans and associated spawning streams; landlocked in some large lakes

Range: Atlantic Coast from Maine to northern Florida, Gulf Coast from Florida to Texas, introduced elsewhere; in Ohio, the Ohio River and Buckeye, Charles Mill, East Fork and Kiser reservoirs, Deer Creek Lake

Food: small fish

Reproduction: spawns in late spring to early summer in freshwater streams; eggs deposited in riffles over gravel bars at the mouth of large tributaries; eggs must remain suspended to hatch

Average Size: 18 to 30 inches, 10 to 20 pounds

Records: state—37 pounds, 2 ounces, West Branch Reservoir, 1993; North American—(inland) 67 pounds, 1 ounces Colorado River, Arizona, 1997

Notes: The Striped Bass is a saltwater fish that migrates into freshwater to spawn. In the early 1960s it was learned that Striped Bass can live entirely in freshwater. Large numbers were stocked into many large southern and western lakes and rivers. These introduced populations cannot reproduce naturally. Since it was first stocked in the 80s this fast-growing, hard-fighting fish has been very popular in Ohio. In recent years stocking has shifted to hybrid Striped Bass that survive better in Ohio's warm water.

Description: olive to blackish green back; silver-green sides, with no stripes except lateral line; front spiny dorsal fin connected by small low membrane to soft-rayed back portion

Similar Species: Striped Bass (pg. 170), Hybrid Striped Bass (pg. 166), White Bass (pg. 168)

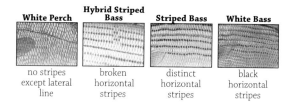

White Perch	Hybrid Striped Bass	Striped Bass	White Bass
no stripes except lateral line	broken horizontal stripes	distinct horizontal stripes	black horizontal stripes

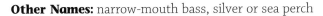

WHITE PERCH

Morone americana

Other Names: narrow-mouth bass, silver or sea perch

Habitat: brackish water, coastal areas of the Great Lakes; expanding range into smaller fresh-water lakes

Range: Mississippi River drainage south to the Gulf of Mexico, Atlantic Coast from Maine to South Carolina; in Ohio, Lake Erie and a few inland lakes

Food: fish eggs in spring and early summer, minnows, insects, crustaceans

Reproduction: spawning takes place in late spring over gravel bars of tributary streams

Average Size: 6 to 8 inches, 1 pound or less

Records: state—1 pound, 7 ounces, Green Creek, 1988; North American—4 pounds, 12 ounces, Messalonskee Lake, Maine, 1949

Notes: The White Perch is a coastal Atlantic species that entered Lake Erie in Ohio in the 1950s. The inland form of this brackish water fish is quickly expanding its range, often in places were it is unwanted. Fish eggs make up 100 percent of its diet in the spring and it has been linked to Walleye declines in some Canadian waters. White Perch are a popular panfish in some parts of the Great Lakes and are commercially harvested in western Lake Erie but are a detriment in many small lakes.

Description: back and sides yellow-brown with slight cross-hatching; dark lateral stripe through lips to tail; slender fish with pelvic, dorsal and anal fins set well back on body; tail, dorsal and anal fins spotted; long snout flattened on top; rounded tail; upturned mouth

Similar Species: Brook Silverside (pg. 120), Central Mudminnow (pg. 80)

Blackstripe Topminnow	**Brook Silverside**	**Central Mudminnow**
front of dorsal behind anal fin origin	two dorsal fins	front of dorsal ahead of anal fin origin

BLACKSTRIPE TOPMINNOW

Fundulidae

Fundulus notatus

Other Names: blackband topminnow

Habitat: slow-moving streams; quiet margins and backwaters of medium-size rivers; small lakes and ponds

Range: southern Great Lakes through the central Mississippi River drainage to the Gulf of Mexico; prairie portions of central and northwest Ohio

Food: insects, crustaceans

Reproduction: spawns when water reaches low 70s F; pairs establish territories along stream edges; male aggressively defends territory; eggs sink to the bottom and are left without parental care

Average Size: 2 to 3 inches

Records: none

Notes: As the name implies "topminnows" inhabit the upper water column and are adapted to feeding on or near the surface. Though inconspicuous and well camouflaged they are a favorite target of wading birds. Blackstripe Topminnows were native to the prairie streams in Ohio. They tolerate turbid (cloudy) water well and are now becoming common in man-made farm ponds—where they are fun to watch always turning into the waves. Though not very colorful they make good aquarium fish that readily eat food spread on the water surface.

Description: silvery-brown back and sides; horizontal rows of dark blotches; adipose fin; single dorsal fin with 2 weak spines and 10 to 11 soft rays; small scales that feel rough

Similar Species: Yellow Perch (pg. 92); Walleye (pg. 90)

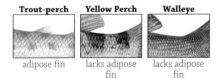

Trout-perch	Yellow Perch	Walleye
adipose fin	lacks adipose fin	lacks adipose fin

TROUT·PERCH

Percopsis omiscomaycus

Other Names: grounder, sand minnow

Habitat: clear to slightly turbid (cloudy) deep lakes and streams with sand or gravel bottoms; avoids soft-bottom shallows

Range: east-central U.S. south to Kansas, North Canada and west to Alaska; Lake Erie and the unglaciated half of Ohio

Food: insects, zooplankton, crustaceans, small fish

Reproduction: migrates from deep water to shorelines and tributary streams when water temperatures reach high 60s F; spawns over gravel or rocks, leaving eggs to hatch with no parental care

Average Size: 2 to 4 inches

Records: none

Notes: There are only two species of Trout-perch and they are restricted to freshwaters of North America. Trout-perch are deep-water fish that are seldom seen unless they wash up on a beach where they are often confused with small Walleyes. They have a nocturnal migration and on some nights large numbers enter the shallows to feed. Trout-perch are an important forage species for game fish and can be a good baitfish. However, seining is only productive in shallow water at night.

GLOSSARY

adipose fin a small, fleshy fin without rays, located on the midline of the fish's back between the dorsal fin and the tail

air bladder a balloon-like organ located in the gut area of a fish, used to control buoyancy—and in the respiration of some species such as gar; also called "swim bladder" or "gas bladder"

alevin a newly hatched fish that still has its yolk sac

anadromous a fish that hatches in freshwater, migrates to the ocean, then re-enters streams or rivers from the sea (or large inland body of water) to spawn

anal fin a single fin located on the bottom of the fish near the tail

annulus marks or rings on the scales, spine, vertebrae or otoliths that scientists use to determine a fish's age

anterior toward the front of a fish, opposite of posterior

bands horizontal marks running lengthwise along the side of a fish

barbel thread-like sensory structures on a fish's head often near the mouth, commonly called "whiskers;" used for taste or smell

bars vertical markings on the side of a fish

benthic organisms living in or on the bottom

brood swarm large group of young fish such as bullheads

cardiform teeth small teeth on the lips of a catfish

carnivore a fish that feeds on other fish or animals

catadromous a fish that lives in freshwater and migrates into saltwater to spawn, such as the American Eel

caudal fin tail fin

caudal peduncle the portion of the fish's body located between the anal fin and the beginning of the tail

coldwater referring to a species or environment; in fish, often a species of trout or salmon found in water that rarely exceeds 70 degrees F; also used to describe a lake or river according to average summer temperature

copepod a small (less than 2 mm) crustacean that is part of the zooplankton community

crustacean a crayfish, water flea, crab or other animal belonging to group of mostly aquatic species that have paired antennae, jointed legs and an exterior skeleton (exoskeleton); common food for many fish

dorsal relating to the top of the fish, on or near the back; opposite of the ventral, or lower, part of the fish

dorsal fin the fin or fins located along the top of a fish's back

eddy a circular water current, often created by an obstruction

epilimnion the warm, oxygen-rich upper layer of water in a thermally stratified lake

exotic a foreign species, not native to a watershed

fingerling a juvenile fish, generally 1 to 10 inches in length, in its first year of life

fork length the overall length of a fish from the mouth to the deepest part of the tail notch

fry recently hatched young fish that have absorbed their yolk sacs

game fish a species regulated by laws for recreational fishing

gills organs used in aquatic respiration

gill cover large bone covering the gills, also called opercle or operculum

gill raker a comblike projection from the gill arch

harvest fish that are caught and kept by sport or commercial anglers

hypolimnion bottom layer of water in a thermally stratified lake (common in summer), usually depleted of oxygen by decaying matter

ichthyologist a scientist who studies fish

invertebrates animals without backbones, such as insects, crayfish, leeches and earthworms

lateral line a series of pored scales along the side of a fish that contain organs used to detect vibrations

littoral zone the part of a lake that is less than 15 feet in depth; this important and often vulnerable area holds the majority of aquatic plants, is a primary area used by young fish, and offers essential spawning habitat for most warmwater fishes such as Walleye and Largemouth Bass

mandible lower jaw

maxillary upper jaw

milt semen of a male fish that fertilizes the female's eggs during spawning

mollusk an invertebrate with a smooth, soft body such as a clam or a snail

native an indigenous or naturally occurring species

omnivore a fish or animal that eats plants and animal matter

otolith an L-shaped bone found in the inner ear of fish

opercle bone covering the gills, also called gill cover or operculum

panfish small freshwater game fish that can be fried whole in a pan, such as crappies, perch and sunfish

pectoral fins paired fins on the side of the fish just behind the gills

pelagic fish species that live in open water, in the food-rich upper layer of water; not associated with the bottom

pelvic fins paired fins below or behind the pectoral fins on the bottom (ventral portion) of the fish

pharyngeal teeth tooth-like structures in the throat on the margins of the gill bars

pheremone a chemical scent secreted as a means of communication between members of the same species

piscivore a predatory fish that mainly eats other fish

planktivore a fish that feeds on plankton

plankton floating or weakly swimming aquatic plants and animals, including larval fish, that drift with the current; often eaten by fish; individual organisms are called plankters

plankton bloom a marked increase in the amount of plankton due to favorable conditions such as nutrients and light

range the geographic region in which a species is found

ray hard supporting part of the fin; resembles a spine but is jointed (can be raised and lowered) and is barbed; found in catfish, carp and goldfish

ray soft flexible structures supporting the fin membrane, sometimes branched

redd a nest-like depression made by a male or female fish during the spawn, often refers to nest of trout and salmon species

riparian area land adjacent to streams, rivers, lakes and other wetlands where the vegetation is influenced by the great availability of water

riprap rock or concrete used to protect a lake shore or river bank from erosion

roe fish eggs

scales small, flat plates covering the outer skin of many fish

Secchi disk a black-and-white circular disk used to measure water clarity; scientists record the average depth at which the disk disappears from sight when lowered into the water

silt small, easily disturbed bottom particles smaller than sand but larger than clay

siltation the accumulation of soil particles

spawning the process of fish reproduction; involves females laying eggs and males fertilizing them to produce young fish

spine stiff, pointed structures found along with soft rays in some fins; unlike hard rays they are not jointed

spiracle an opening on the posterior portion of the head above and behind the eye

standard length length of the fish from the mouth to the end of the vertebral column

stocking the purposeful, artificial introduction of a fish species into an area

substrate bottom composition of a lake, stream or river

subterminal mouth below the snout of the fish

swim bladder see air bladder

tailrace area immediately downstream of a dam or power plant

tapetum lucidum reflective pigment in a Walleye's eye

thermocline middle layer of water in a stratified lake, typically oxygen rich, characterized by a sharp drop in water temperature; often the lowest depth at which fish can be routinely found

terminal mouth forward facing

total length the length of the fish from the mouth to the tail compressed to its fullest length

tributary a stream that feeds into another stream, river or lake

turbid cloudy; water clouded by suspended sediments or plant matter that limits visibility and the passage of light

velocity the speed of water flowing in a stream or river

vent the opening at the end of the digestive tract

ventral the underside of the fish

vertebrate an animal with a backbone

vomerine teeth teeth on the roof of the mouth

warmwater a non-salmonid species of fish that lives in water that routinely exceeds 70 degrees F; also used to describe a lake or river according to average summer temperature

yolk the part of an egg containing food for the developing fish

zooplankton the animal component of plankton; tiny animals that float or swim weakly; common food of fry and small fish

PRIMARY REFERENCES

Becker, G. C. 1983
Fishes of Wisconsin
University of Wisconsin Press

Hubbs, C. L. and Lagler, K. F. revised by Smith, G. R 2004
Fishes of the Great Lakes Region
University of Michigan Press

McClane, A. J. 1978
Freshwater Fishes of North America
Henry Holt and Company

Thomas, P. assisted by Callahan, E. 2004
Lake Erie Fish Illustrated
Allegheny Press Science Series No. 28

Trautman, M. B. 1957
The Fishes of Ohio
Ohio State University Press

Werner, R. G. 2004
Freshwater Fishes of the Northeastern States
Syracuse University Press

INDEX

ABOUT THE AUTHOR

Dave Bosanko was born in Kansas and studied engineering before following his love of nature to degrees in biology and chemistry from Emporia State University. He spent thirty years as staff biologist at two of the University of Minnesota's field stations. Though his training was in mammal physiology, Dave worked on a wide range of research projects ranging from fish, bird and mammal population studies to experiments with biodiversity and prairie restoration. An avid fisherman and naturalist, he has long enjoyed applying the fruits of his extensive field research to patterning fish location and behavior, and observing how these fascinating species interact with one another in the underwater web of life.